Behavioral Consulting:

Improving Client and Consultee Learning and Behavior

G. Roy Mayer
San Diego State University

Michele Wallace
California State University, Los Angeles

2020
Sloan Publishing
Cornwall on Hudson, NY 12520

Library of Congress Control Number: 9781597380935.

Cover photo: sandboxsuites.com

© 2020 by Sloan Publishing, LLC

Sloan Publishing, LLC
220 Maple Road
Cornwall-on-Hudson, NY 12520

All rights reserved. No portion of this book may be reproduced, in any form or by any means, without permission in writing from the Publisher.

Printed in the United States of America

10 9 8 7 6 5 4 3 2 1

ISBN 13: 978-1-59738-093-5
ISBN 10: 1-59738-093-8

Contents

1. **An Orientation to Behavioral Consulting**   1
   Behavioral Consulting Defined   2
   Why Consulting?   3
   Types of Consultant Relationships   6
   Factors Influencing Your Effectiveness as a Consultant   7
   Summary and Conclusions   12

2. **Developing Rapport and Collaborative Relationships**   15
   Professional Communication Skills   16
   Multiculturalism—Diversity and Equity in Consultation   25
   Actions to Avoid   29
   Summary and Conclusions   30

3. **Interfacing and Consulting with the Medical Profession**   33
   by *Linda Copeland and Greg Buch*
   Medical History at Intake   34
   The Possible Impact of Medical Conditions During Behavioral Interventions   36
   Behaviors Indicating Possible Medical Conditions   37
   Determining Behavior's Communicative Intent with Clients Who Have Limited Speaking Skills   38
   Making the Medical Referral   40
   Other Areas Behavior Specialists Might Consult Regarding Medical Conditions   40
   A Closer Look at Consultation: Multidisciplinary Examples   41
   Summary and Conclusions   44

4. **Promoting Implementation with Fidelity**   46
   Address Resistance to Implementing the Intervention   46
   Additional Strategies for Enhancing Fidelity of Implementation   52
   Summary and Conclusions   64

5. Determining Fidelity of Implementation   66
   Operationally Defining Correct and Incorrect Implementation   66
   Measuring and Reporting Treatment Integrity   69
   What to Do About Integrity Failures   74
   Summary and Conclusions   75

6. Promoting Continued Implementation   76
   Provide Feedback   77
   Ensure Environmental Support and Reinforcement   85
   Summary and Conclusions   90

7. Helping Consultees "Make It on Their Own": Maintenance and Generalization   92
   Reducing Prompts   92
   Reducing Reinforcers   93
   Promoting Generalization   95
   Major Points for Promoting Generalization and Maintenance   96
   Summary and Conclusions   96

8. Assessing Consultation Effectiveness   97
   Measuring at the Client Level   97
   Measuring at the Consultee Level   100
   Measuring at the Consultant Level   103
   Summary and Conclusions   105

Appendix   107
References   111

Preface

We are pleased to share the consulting knowledge we have accumulated over the years from not only our own training, research, and experience, but also from our students and the work of numerous other professionals, many of whom are cited in this book. We hope, and believe, that the material you are about to read will enhance your effectiveness as a consultant.

Having taught from other books we have written (*Behavior analysis for lasting change, 4th ed.,* by Mayer, Sulzer-Azaroff, & Wallace, 2019—a book for preparing Board Certified Behavior Analysts (BCBAs); and *Principles of applied behavior analysis: For behavior technicians and other practitioners, 2nd ed.,* by Wallace & Mayer, 2019), and from our own consulting and observing others consultants, we discovered *a considerable need for a book that addresses consulting skills.*

BCBAs and other professionals (school psychologists, speech therapists and many others) have been taught applied behavior analysis, and have been implementing programs for decades. However, it has become apparent that if programs are to be implemented by paraprofessionals, such as Registered Behavior Technicians (RBTs), classroom aides, employee supervisors, and others, *how one consults with paraprofessionals can determine the degree of programs' achieved fidelity* (i.e., if the intervention programs are implemented as designed). Moreover, as the field of behavior analysis goes beyond educational and clinical practice, the need to understand consultation from a behavior analytic perspective is evident.

Through effective consultation, you can help others learn to acquire new skills and behaviors that will assist them in moving toward achieving their goals and potential in working with their children, students, or employees. Effective consultation skills, as inferred above, can help promote fidelity of implementation (i.e., enhance the likelihood that your intervention programs will be implemented by RBTs [Registered Behavioral Technicians], supervisors, parents, teachers, and others as you have designed them). Thus, *effective consultation skills are critical to the success of most behavior interventions,* and the reason why we have written this book. We hope you will use it to help improve your skills in helping others, your consultees, and implementing behavior interventions.

A Note to Instructors

Sample multiple choice items and **power point presentations** for each chapter can be obtained (given proper bona fides) directly from the publisher at info@sloanpublishing.com. Also, activities are provided at the end of each chapter that can be assigned to help students further understand and use behavioral consultation.

Acknowledgements

Many of the ideas and examples for explaining topics have come from the thousand of interactions the authors have had with students as well as practicing professionals. We are especially thankful for Lucy Ainsman, BCBA, Clinical Behavioral Supervisor at Xcite Steps, Benjamin N. Witts (St. Cloud State University), and Katina Lambros (San Diego State University) for their helpful feedback on an earlier version of this book.

Roy dedicates this book to his family and Joyce Ahern for their love and support. Michele, dedicates this book to Jay Wallace (the best father ever), Tymerie Busser (wife), Payton (daughter), Aiden (son), Margaret Garcia (BFF, chosen sister); and all the Bussers, Sims, and Seymours for their love, support, and tons of encouragement.

About the Authors

G. Roy Mayer, Ed.D., BCBA-D is Professor Emeritus at California State University, Los Angeles. He obtained his doctorate at Indiana University in 1966, taught at Southern Illinois University for three years, and then at CSULA for about 30 years. In 2008, he also served as Visiting Professor at NamSeoul University, South Korea. Dr. Mayer is one of the co-founders of Cal-ABA, served as its Program Co-Chairman and President, and received recognition from Cal-ABA as an Outstanding Contributor to Behavior Analysis. He also was recognized with the Outstanding Professor Award from CSULA. He has served on various editorial boards, has published numerous behavioral articles, and published a number of chapters and books (including one book that was translated into Korean and two into Spanish). He has given over 100 presentations, including several keynote addresses, has served as consultant to various school districts, and supervised in-home RBTs. He also has life-time California Service Credentials in counseling, school psychology, social work, and child welfare and attendance. Currently, he teaches ABA part-time at San Diego State University, enjoys teaching others about ABA through his writing and teaching, and enjoys his family and the San Diego weather.

Michele D. Wallace Ph.D., BCBA-D is a full time professor at California State University, Los Angeles and is the program director for the Applied Behavior Analysis Program. Dr. Michele Wallace graduated from the University of Florida in 2000 with her doctorate in the Experimental Analysis of Behavior under the guidance of Dr. Brian Iwata. Dr. Wallace has served on the Board of Editors for the *Journal of Applied Behavior Analysis* and has served as a guest reviewer for many other behavioral journals. She has been a Board Certified Behavior Analyst in the State of Florida since 1993 and a National Board Certified Behavior Analyst since 2000. Dr. Wallace has served on various professional boards including the Nevada Association for Behavior Analysis, California Association for Behavior Analysis, and the Behavior Analysis Certification Board. In addition, she has served as a behavior consultant to many agencies and school districts all over the United States and in China and Taiwan. She has authored and co-authored books, chapters, articles, and numerous presentations. Finally, she is the proud behavioral mom of two amazing children (Payton and Aiden).

Chapter 1

An Orientation to Behavioral Consulting

What does the word consultation mean? One possible definition of consultation is "a meeting with an expert or professional to seek advice." Consultation is generally agreed to be a situation or process in which an individual receives information, advice, assistance, or services from a consultant (aka a professional). Usually the consultant is someone with specific knowledge or skills that are relevant to the identification and solution of a specific problem (Williams, 2000). Consulting is not a new activity. It occurs in all walks of life. For hundreds of years, world leaders have surrounded themselves with advisors or counselors to either help them make decisions or jointly make decisions. Attorneys consult with their clients; investors with their investment advisors; school administrations, psychologist, counselors, and resource specialists with each other, and Behavior Analysts with teachers, parents, and other professionals (e.g., speech therapists, occupational therapists, medical doctors, real estate agents, factory owners, etc.). Supervisors consult with their staff or employees, and on and on the list goes. One could argue that, *consultants seek to assist and maintain others to competently and effectively achieve their goals.* In fact, given this definition, one could argue that most work one does in applied behavior analysis falls under behavior consultation regardless of whether the behavior analyst is working in the home, school, department of rehabilitation, a factory, or an organization. Williams (2000) has stated, "behavioral consultation would be defined as bringing about socially validated solutions to a) others' problems in ways that are b) empirically defined, c) analytical, d) technological, e) conceptually systematic, f) effective, and g) that show generality" (p. 377).

Because of a focus on current research, the present direction in our field appears to overlook many important early studies on consultation that have occurred within our field, and related fields, since its inception. They are included because their findings are very relevant to our understanding of the consultant-consultee relationship. Because of this, we have made a point of incorporating such work throughout this book, often interweaving them with core current studies.

BEHAVIORAL CONSULTING DEFINED

In contrast to many other approaches to consulting, **Behavioral Consulting** *seeks to assist others in achieving their goals by using learning principles or findings from experimental and applied research.* Moreover, behavioral consulting is not just about providing advice or teaching someone new tricks, but teaching them how to view the situation from a behavior analytic point of view and developing and implementing evidence-based solutions. Behavioral consulting, as we use it, is the act of conferring with **consultees** (e.g., *teachers, parents, peers, Registered Behavioral Technicians, [RBTs], and other staff or employees in various institutions and organizations who are responsible for a person's behavior*) regarding the effects that their behavior and provided environment have on an individual's behavior/learning (i.e., client). Behavioral consulting involves helping consultees use behavioral information to formulate objectives and to select behavioral procedures to be used in facilitating the client's learning and personal-social development. Behavioral consulting also goes beyond helping or teaching consultees about applied behavior analysis (ABA). It seeks to actively engage consultees in a partnership from which to problem-solve from an ABA framework. And, it frequently uses research or evidence-based strategies within the consultation process. For example, research shows that to be maximally effective, the consultant needs to provide on-going feedback and support, not just one or more information sessions or workshops, as the consultee is learning new behavioral skills. (Specifics of this component are described in Chapter 6.)

Behavioral consultants seek to enhance the competencies of consultees in helping others move toward the attainment of their goals as well as informing them of how to evaluate the environmental contributions to a situation. To do so, the same behavioral learning principles and procedures used in changing or teaching individuals various behaviors are used in the consulting relationship. As Mayer (1972) pointed out years ago, behavioral procedures are as applicable to the consultant-teacher, consultant-parent or consultant-supervisor relationship as they are to the teacher-student or parent-child, or any interpersonal relationships, such as counselor or psychologist with teacher, youngster, or parent, Board Certified Behavior Analysts (BCBAs) with RBTs, or administrator/supervisor with teacher or employee. It is the specific stimuli (i.e., objects or events) within each behavioral procedure that vary among relationships. For example, a behavioral consultant is more likely to use praise than hugs or computer time as a reinforcer with teachers and parents, though he or she might recommend such reinforcers with a child, but the process for achieving the behavior change is the same (positive reinforcement). As we will illustrate, reinforcement procedures, as well as many other behavioral procedures, are applicable to all interpersonal relationships. Basically then, a good consultant has learned to apply the same ABA skills learned for working with **clients** (*the individuals whose behavior is targeted for change, usually a child, student, subject, patient, or employee*) to the consultant-consultee relationship. This book is designed to help you generalize those skills from the client to the consultee. However, before delving into the consulting relationship, let's discuss why consulting is an important professional activity.

WHY CONSULTING?

Below, we present five major reasons why consulting activities are emphasized by behaviorists. You will note, these are not new concepts.

The Influence of Significant Others

Significant others in the life of individuals (i.e., *those who have frequent contact with them such as parents, teachers, or supervisors*) teach and influence behavior in a variety of positive and negative ways. Research by pioneers in the field of Behavior Analysis, such as Gerald Patterson and Vance Hall, have taught us that many children and youth do not pay attention or follow directions, engage in disruptive activities, and behave in other ways that interfere with their learning. This may be because they have been taught to behave that way by significant others. Classmates, teachers, and parents have all been shown to inadvertently reinforce disruptive, deviant behavior (Buehler, Patterson, & Furness, 1966). Even nursery school children have been noted to reinforce approximately 70 percent of the aggressive responses of their peers (Patterson, Littman, & Bricker, 1967). Such research findings indicate that behavioral consultation must include informing parents, teachers, peers, and others of the effects that their behavior and provided environments have on others; and, the consultant needs to help them use this information effectively. Given the generality of behavior analysis procedures and processes it is not unfathomable to realize the effects that adults have on another adult's behavior as well. For example, it would be easy to think of a situation when you have "accidentally" reinforced the inappropriate behavior of a supervisor or co-worker by reinforcing their behavior to get out of the aversiveness of a situation. Thankfully, research shows that when significant others have participated in behavioral consulting as consultees, client behavior has improved considerably (e.g., Farber & Mayer, 1980; Mayer et al., 1983; 1993; Arco, 1997; Dengerink,

2014). Because significant others are a vital part of an individual's environment, modifying their behavior can directly influence the client's behavior.

Let's look at a couple of sample studies: Although direct services with children may sound like the best approach to changing behavior, an early study on this topic by Taylor and Hoedt (1974) indicated that this is not the case. They compared the effects of directly implementing treatment with children to training significant adults (parents and teachers) to implement treatment. In analyzing the results of 372 elementary school children, they concluded that the significant others were more effective in reducing behavior problems than directed services to the child, regardless of grade level. Dengerink (2014) found that once in-home consultation was provided to parents following workshop training, parents significantly increased their approving statements and decreased their disapproving comments or actions. These changes in turn, were shown to relate to significant increases in child compliance.

The manpower it would take to change every child's behavior or employee's behavior would be an enormous endeavor; however, teaching the significant others (parent of multiple kids, teacher of a classroom with 20+ students, manager of 50+ employees, etc.) does seem like a prudent solution. Moreover, such findings seem reasonable, as it is not the professional counselor, therapist, social worker, CEO, or others who will effectively manage an individual's behavior, but it is the significant others who are, in most cases, in the best position to most effectively change the behavior. It is also the *significant others who usually determine the long-term effects of most any behavioral change program*. Professionals usually control far fewer and less powerful reinforcers than do the significant others. Thus, significant others are in a position to have a more powerful influence on an individual's behavior than outside professionals, and thus usually serve as our consultees.

Prevention

Behavioral consultants inform significant others of the effects that their behaviors and environment are having on others. They follow up with helping the significant others to use this information to formulate objectives and to select behavioral procedures to facilitate the learning and personal-social development of others. By enhancing the competencies of significant others in facilitating social and academic growth, the consultant seeks to reduce the number of people needing individual services. Significant others are taught strategies that can be used not only for immediate problem situations, but also to facilitate their own and others' learning and personal-social development in future situations.

A number of years ago (1972), Paul Clement emphasized the preventive nature of behavioral consulting by pointing out that once significant others are trained in the use of specific aspects of the behavioral approach, their "competence and confidence to deal effectively with present and future problems are increased" p. 17). The ultimate outcome of training significant others is that they learn what creates, maintains, and eliminates behavioral problems and how to overcome skill deficits and teach new skills effectively. Hence, the whole approach emphasized prevention of future difficulties. Thus, teaching general and foundational knowledge of behavior analysis promotes the potential of significant others' applying these strategies when reacting to the occurrence of unexpected behavior that do not have a behavior protocol in place.

Stimulus Generalization

A behavior has generalized when it occurs in a situation other than the one in which it was learned, at different times of day, and in the presence of different people. The greater the similarity between two situations, the greater the likelihood that generalization will occur in that there is a greater chance that discriminative stimuli (cues, prompts) that were in the situation in which the behavior was learned are also in the similar situation to prompt the behavior's occurrence. A basic, but not always valid, assumption implicit in direct services (i.e., behavior therapist to client) is that a behavior or skill learned in that context will generalize or transfer to other settings, other people, or other behaviors without any additional effort. Yet, the therapeutic context is usually very different from all other contexts. Therapy often occurs in an office with an adult working with a client or a small group of clients. Such a situation is very different from what occurs in the home, classroom, or factory. Thus, generalization training is often necessary to help clients generalize the behavior to other settings or persons. Behavioral consultation can be viewed as a form of generalization training in that it teaches the consultee (behavior change agent) how to respond to similar situations without additional training. For example, in behavioral consultation with a parent, the parent is taught how to not only respond to Mark (her son) but can generalize her skills and be an effective contingency manager with her daughter, employee, and yes, even her spouse. Also, because the skills are being taught in the natural environment, generalization of behavior from the therapy office to the natural environment does not need to be taught. Or perhaps the manager, who has received behavioral consultation to effectively manage their employees' productivity, can generalize their skills to effectively manage their employees' on-time arrival. So, usually, *less generalization training is needed when using behavioral consultation as compared to private therapy or counseling.*

Cost and Time

Behavioral consulting is less time-consuming and costly than conducting and implementing individualized behavior change programs. For example, if we wanted to decrease unsafe behavior in a factory, we could implement an individualized plan for every worker, or we could consult with management and institute some behavior programs throughout the factory and monitor and reinforce safe behavior. Moreover, it is best to implement interventions throughout a client's waking day. (One or two sessions per a week is usually insufficient.) Because daily treatment is usually in the best interests of the client, it is much more economical to teach significant others to augment existing resources. The cost of a professional delivering such programs would be prohibitive in time and money. The competencies and confidence of the significant others are enhanced by consulting. And, as you help teachers and parents improve their skills in teaching and managing behavior, they can use those skills that they learned working with one or two youngsters on many other youngsters throughout their lives. Similarly, managers are able to use what you have taught them throughout their careers to deal with decreasing absences and other behaviors within the factory (e.g., production, promptness, work satisfaction).

Treatment Integrity

It is not enough to teach behavioral interventions to consultees, but as a behavioral consultant you need to help ensure that the interventions are being implemented with fidelity: That is, is the intervention *being implemented correctly*? Generally, given a well-designed plan of intervention, *the higher the treatment integrity, the more effective the intervention*. As behavioral consultants you have the responsibility of assuring that agreed-to interventions are being implemented correctly. On-going behavioral consultations *help to assure treatment integrity* in that consultants can observe and give feedback during their consultation visits. (Topics we elaborate on throughout this book.)

TYPES OF CONSULTANT RELATIONSHIPS

There are three types of consultant-consultee relationships: *Expert*, the *pair-of-hands*, and *collaborative* (Block, 1981). In the **expert role**, *the consultant is hired based upon their knowledge within a specific area* (e.g., a behavior analyst who specializes in feeding disorders). In the **pair-of-hands role**, *the consultant is usually hired to complete a specific task* (e.g., a behavior analyst hired to implement a safety program in a factory). In a **collaborative role**, *the consultant and the consultee work together to define the problem and develop solutions* (e.g., a behavior analyst and a classroom teacher working together to develop an effective classroom management program). The latter is usually the most preferred method of consultation. The collaborative role is argued to provide the consultant sufficient influence, and the consultee is more likely to assume responsibility and commitment to change. There are a number of factors that contribute to the type and effectiveness of consultation.

FACTORS INFLUENCING YOUR EFFECTIVENESS AS A CONSULTANT[1]

Behavioral consultants do not work in a vacuum. There are a variety of factors at the consulting site that can affect your effectiveness. Thus, it is important for you to assess such factors before you begin your consulting. Consultants who accurately assess the external and internal environmental and organizational factors that can affect their ability to provide services will be in a better position to create lasting change than those who do not assess those factors. By assessing environmental barriers to services, you can often modify the environment before implementing programs for behavior change and decrease its conflicting and aversive effect on services. Similarly, the type of professional interpersonal relationships you develop with consultees are critical to your effectiveness. Rosenfield (1991) has argued that the relationship between consultee and consultant is underestimated in its importance for successful outcomes. Thus, it would be amiss for a book on consultation to not address such an important relationship. Below we point out some of the external and internal factors of which you should be aware in the setting in which you might work.

External Factors

HOME. A variety of external factors affecting the home environment can affect your consulting effectiveness. What influence does job demands or job satisfaction have on the home environment? Are there conflicts or expectations by relatives or neighbors that are influencing the parents' interactions with one another or with their children? Are drugs an issue? What sort of relationships do the children have with other children in the neighborhood or with their cousins? Are there conflicts or pressures associated with adult "friends?" What are the social-economical factors affecting the family? Factors such as these can have a major impact in your effectiveness when consulting with parents.

SCHOOL. Most schools in the United States tend to operate semi-independently. However, there are a number of individuals, groups, and organizations that frequently exert pressure on the school. Parent or community groups, service clubs, central administration, school board members, and other influential community members all provide input into the school environment, affecting its operation. You need to become aware of their influence and goals to help you become aware of some of the constrains within which you must work. If important groups in the community or central administration are leery of change and

---

[1] Many of the following factors are based on those originally presented by Mayer and McGookin (1997)

innovative programs, you will need to proceed in a more cautious fashion that you might otherwise have chosen.

Perhaps the most important external variable is the central administration. Does it approve of and support the use of behavioral strategies? If not, you will find difficulty implementing programs. Sometimes the lack of support by the central administration is due to the type of reinforcers that others have used in the past. If so, make it clear that you will not be using those particular reinforcers without permission. Also, it often is helpful to discover the school principal's status with the central administrator. Is the principal regarded positively or negatively? If negatively, behavioral programs developed in that school are less likely to be recommended to other schools.

COMPANY. How independent is the company? Is there a board of directors and/or stock holders? If so, what are their goals and how do they compliment the company's stated goals and purpose? How does the company collaborate with other companies? What sort of reputation does it have in the community, with consumer advocacy organizations, and on-line review platforms (e.g., Yelp® and Google®)? What has contributed to their reputation? What is the mission of the company or what does the strategic plan say? All of these factors (and additional ones not mentioned here) can influence the consultation outcomes.

Internal Factors

HOME. Understanding the situation that you will be working in can prove very helpful to how you might approach various topics and suggestions. Factors in the home that can be helpful to address include: How does each parent feel about the use of behavioral interventions with their child, such as reinforcing appropriate behavior? Are both parents on the same page, or do they disagree as to the type of programs that should be implemented? Is there much conflict between the parents? Do they have specific concerns about any aspect of a behavioral program? (If so, you will need to address them, because if they are not aboard with the intervention, the program is not likely to be successful over time. See Chapter 4 as to common concerns and how to address them.) What is their approach to teaching and disciplining their children? Does any member of the family have any psychological or medical diagnosis or drug issues that may affect their behavior? What are their cultural beliefs about parenting and family?

SCHOOL. Schools have a number of internal factors that are helpful to be aware of, including organizational structure, the personnel, and the staff's expectations and biases.

Become aware of the *organizational structure*, or day-to-day running of the school, including how and by whom are decisions made. When the principal is not present, who has the authority to act in his or her place? What are the relationships among teachers within a grade level and across grade levels? How does one obtain support services and resources? How are problems identified, strategies implemented, and results evaluated? The following example, shared by a colleague (Roger McGookin) illustrates the importance of the consultant's awareness of the school's structure:

> A consultant (a school psychologist) was on a school's campus working with a teacher in the classroom. An urgent call came from the office requesting his help. A student had been sent to the office for throwing chairs at his teacher. The secretary asked the consultant to talk to the student. He talked to the student and helped calm him down. A call was then made to the student's home, but his parents could not be contacted. The consultant then suggested that the boy spend the remainder of the day with one of the male teachers. Later, a series of negative side effects occurred. When the teacher who had sent the boy to the office asked what had happened to him, she was told that he was transferred to Mr. Kee's room. When the principal returned to the campus the next day, the teacher complained bitterly about having the boy suddenly removed from her classroom. The principal, assuming that the consultant usurped his authority, became angry. The relationship the consultant had worked for two months to develop with the school staff and principal was almost destroyed in just a few minutes.

The difficulty above could have been avoided if the consultant had known who was responsible in the principal's absence, and with whom he needed to communicate.

One of the most important variables affecting the outcome of a consultant's work are the *personnel* involved in the school activities: The principal, teachers, secretaries, lunch and recess monitors, and parent leaders.

Learn how the *principal's* orientation, administrative style, decision-making patterns, and relations with central administration, faculty, and community affect all aspects of the school. Also, determine what sort of teacher and student behavior he reinforces and what sort he punishes, including their frequency and what reinforcers and punishers are used (e.g., assignment of duties, student load and student behavior issues, class materials, approval/disapproval, privileges, schedules). If the principal tends to reinforce the behavior of certain teachers more than others, determine if it would be possible to use them as models. It may also be necessary to point out to the principal the effect that the punishment is having on behavior of students and teachers. The principal's reliance on punishment may be imitated by teachers, resulting in their using more of it on their students' behaviors.

Do not overlook the *school secretary* or *administrative assistant*. Frequently this person has been at the school longer than either the principal or the majority of the teaching staff, and is aware of subtle teacher conflicts, impending problems, and school culture. The administrative assistant often acts as a sentry controlling both the inward and outward flow of information and people to the principal. Be sure to get on his or her good side. This person can help you attain access to the principal and various staff, and can help you understand the dynamics within the school.

Regarding *faculty*, identify the formal and informal leaders on the faculty, subgrouping, and whether these groupings are based on loyalties to the principal, age, educational biases, grade level, seniority at the school, or professional organizations. If you find yourself trying to introduce new procedures in a school, capitalize on the influence of prestigious members of the staff by using them to model various behavioral procedures. You may need to select leaders from one or more subgroups to serve as models to maximize the impact and acceptance of various behavioral programs school-wide or even by a specific classroom teacher. Also, recognize that many teacher education programs still do not include training in behavior analysis. As a result, many teachers will neither see nor understand behavioral challenges through a behavioral lens.

In addition, be sure to check out the expectations, beliefs and biases, and the setting in which you are consulting. Too frequently, unwritten and unspoken beliefs determine educational policy. Economically disadvantaged or minority students may be viewed as being incapable of making normal educational advancements. Students coming from affluent backgrounds may be viewed as being over-indulged or spoiled. Special education students are sometimes viewed as having no place in some regular education activities. Others believe that all children in their classroom will automatically want to learn what is taught, and should not be given reinforcement for doing their assigned activities. Parents and/or the principal may be viewed as threats to be avoided whenever possible. It is important for you to ascertain what the hidden beliefs are and how you can work within and begin to change them. With hope, material in this book will help you achieve such tasks (specifically, Chapter 2 provides some suggestions regarding assessing the cultural aspects).

COMPANY. As with schools, you will want to find out the organizational structure of a company, who makes what sort of decisions, and what sort of supervision and support the company provides. For example, will they support continuing education activities and access to behavioral literature? What are their practices in supervising, evaluating, and promoting their employees? Are there any systems in place to promote ethical behavior? How are interpersonal problems handled between supervisors and those being supervised? How are health records and other employee personal information managed?

It is important to ask what the company sees as its major goals and purpose and if they anticipate any changes in the future. If so, what changes? How will your role and activities help them accomplish their goals and purpose? Also, it is important to find out how the company accommodates differences in the cultural backgrounds of their employees and the customers/clients they serve.

The Behavioral Consulting Relationship—Avoid Using Technical Terms

The relationship between the behavioral consultant and consultee often determines the degree of success achieved in solving problems. It is through this relationship that the behavioral strategy and procedures are transmitted to teachers, parents, managers, and additional significant others. Throughout the rest of this book we describe numerous aspects of consulting and various behavioral procedures frequently used in the consulting relationship that can help promote a productive, positive relationship. However, one key point you should be aware of from the beginning is that it is very important to use a *comprehensible language* when talking with your consultees.

When providing instructions and explanations, you must be careful with the terms that you use. Those of us who have training in applied behavior analysis (ABA) have had a number of technical terms drilled into us. These terms have precise meaning, and as a result, we can communicate with one another very effectively without a lot of elaboration to clarify our meaning. However, those we consult with usually do not have much, if any, training in ABA. As a result, the use of terms like discriminative stimuli, negative reinforcement, shaping, chaining, etc., may have not only little meaning to them, but they are likely to find some of the technical terms confusing and frustrating. Critchfield et al. (2017) found "a tendency for behavior analysis terms to register as more unpleasant than other kinds of professional terms and also as more unpleasant than English words generally" (p. 97). We need to recognize that people's emotional reactions are critical to the program's success, and many have a negative emotional reaction to ABA terms.

You need to adjust the language you use with consultees so that it is comprehensible (Binder, 1994; Carr, 1996; Mayer & McGookin, 1977). The importance of using comprehensible language is stressed in the Professional and Ethical Compliance Code by the Behavior Analyst Certification Board®: "Use language that is fully understandable to the recipient of those services" (2016, p. 5). This only makes sense, as good teaching and shaping have taught us to begin at the learners' level of skill or expertise, not where you would like them to be. Similarly, modeling research has taught us to not present a modeled behavior that is too complex. So, at least initially, use terms that your consultee uses (e.g., motivated, self-worth, self-concept, strokes, etc.). A good strategy to use when in an institutional setting, such as a school, is spend some time in the teachers' lounge on several occasions and listen rather than talk to identify the basic orientation and the "in" terminology. Once you have identified the "in" terms, use them, at least initially, when they apply to a situation being discussed. In a home, again listen to what terms the parents use and use them. In an organization, hang out in the break or lunch room. Also, substitute lay terminology for technical terms. See Table 1.1 for Everyday Terms for Technical ABA Terminology. Also, Critchfield (2017) reports that "Visuwords® offers one means of vetting substitute expressions that non experts might find more palatable than jargon" (p. 319).

When communicating with non-behaviorists, Carr (1996) also has pointed out that we should use the language of ethics rather than that of technology. We need to emphasize how the intervention strategies can help promote personal responsibility, freedom, dignity, equality, and justice. The key is to communicate in a language that is not intimidating or off-putting, and that your consultees will understand and accept. When consultees clearly understand exactly what is expected of them and why, they usually improve their performance.

It is also important to remember that some may have a different understanding of specific technical language. For example, a lot of other professions who you might find yourself consulting with believe they know what negative reinforcement is but, in reality, they have a complete misunderstanding of the term. Another common term that is completely misunderstood by others is extinction. It is not uncommon to hear in a school-based meeting that the team feels like they have used extinction, but it hasn't worked. They think extinction means for the teacher to not deliver attention. What they don't realize is that procedurally, extinction depends on the function of the problem behavior (e.g., the function might be to gain peer attention, not teacher attention or to get out of doing work).

It is non-behavioral to use technical language with people who do not understand it.

SUMMARY AND CONCLUSIONS

A behavior consultant will use the principles and procedures of behavior analysis to change the behavior of consultees (often the significant other) so that they can more effectively change the behavior of others (e.g., kids, co-workers, clients). This behavior change will be achieved by systematically assessing the environment and developing and implementing procedures to get behavior change agents to implement evidence-based interventions. The outcomes of effective behavioral consultation are far-reaching and can include great cost savings. It is important to note that there are different possible consultant-consultee relationships and to be aware of factors, such as the language you use, that can either positively or negatively influence these relationships.

TABLE 1.1 Everyday Terms for Technical ABA Terminology*

Technical Term	Alternative Term	Plain English
Reinforcement	Rewarding, giving incentives	Increasing the behavior by praising, attending to, or recognizing accomplishment and effort; providing special rewards, events, and activities; removing nagging or criticism
Stimulus generalization	Transfer	Teaching clients who have learned skills under one condition to apply them under conditions sharing similar qualities
Stimulus change	Environmental change	Teaching clients to act differently under different conditions by changing the environment
Modeling	Demonstrating, showing	Teaching by setting an example; demonstrating a new task or behavior
Shaping and Chaining	Individualized instruction, coaching	Teaching clients by beginning at their current level of performance and breaking down complicated learning tasks or behaviors into smaller parts that they can learn one portion at a time
Fading	Fostering independent learning	Enabling the client to assume increasing independence by helping, reminding, and suggesting less and less often
Scheduling	Developing intrinsic motivation	Assisting the client to increasingly perform the behavior in the absence of rewards, which, in turn, promotes the client's personal satisfaction with accomplishments and achievements
Extinction	Appropriate withholding of reinforcement	Reducing an unwanted behavior by withholding attention or other rewards from behaviors that interfere with constructive learning or performance
Timeout	Temporary separation from the group	Reducing an unwanted behavior to maintain a supportive or safe learning environment by temporarily separating the person from the group to allow him or her to regain self-control and composure, or to protect others from harm
Response Cost	Penalties	Reducing an unwanted behavior by subtracting points, losing yardage, fining
Satiation	Excessive use, consumption, or repetition of a behavior	Reducing an unwanted behavior by providing excessive amounts of rewards or activities, which brings about a reduction in the activity, e.g., eating, shouting, lifting weights.

*The lay language is only illustrative and not representative of all possible types of application of the term. This table was developed by Mayer, Sulzer-Azaroff, and Wallace (2019).

ACTIVITIES

1. Analyze an environment similar to the one you are likely to work in and list (a) internal and (b) external factors that may influence the outcome of your services.
2. Give example of words you will use, and explain why you selected these words in place of specific technical terms, with one of your consultees (select a parent, teacher, or supervisor, or some other person with whom you can practice behavioral consulting while studying this book).

Chapter 2

Developing Rapport and Collaborative Relationships

Promoting change is not easy. Once we become used to doing things in a particular manner, we are apt to maintain that pattern even in the face of our failing to attain our own long-range goals. We may develop eating habits that may defeat our wish to lose weight, or use child-management techniques that work for the moment but inhibit the later development of self-control or long-term behavior change. Sometimes our behavior has become so automatic that we may be unaware that we're engaged in it at the time. Plus, there is the comfort and security of doing things the way we're used to doing them.

Changing such well-established patterns means that we must tolerate the aversiveness of expending considerable time and effort, to say nothing of denying ourselves immediate reinforcement. Following a diet, for example, may require considerable effort and attention as well as the discomfort of forgoing our favorite foods. Helping a consultee (e.g., parent or teacher) to stop yelling at a youth's disruptive attention-seeking behavior that provides immediate reinforcement for yelling, because the attention-seeking antics stop immediately after the yelling, is not easy. Getting them to praise him for being on-task and use extinction to replace the yelling can be even more difficult because extinction can result in punishment of its use. (As you know, the disruptive behavior often increases during the early stages of using extinction. This increase in disruption often serves to punish the continued use of extinction.) Getting a supervisor to add visual prompts of what a safe workplace looks like, and reinforcing the employee when their work station complements the example, is more difficult than the supervisor just sending the employee home for unsafe behavior to avoid another safety accident. The reinforcers for changing behavior are long-range, while reinforcers maintaining our current behavior are NOW—a losing contest, unless certain steps are taken. You must not only be able to communicate your understanding of your consultees' frustrations, but also provide other sources of reinforcement to help them implement the program. *Always be aware of the facts that old ways of behaving can produce more immediate reinforcement than new ways, and learning new ways of behaving can take time and effort (which is often punishing)*.

This chapter focuses on the initial contacts, how to begin to establish rapport and communicate your understanding, and how to include cultural factors into the equation. Later chapters will focus on what you can do to help promote program implementation and maintenance.

The success or failure of your consultation can depend upon how the initial contact is managed with the significant others, such as parents, teachers, and managers/supervisors whom henceforth we will call **consultees**—*those significant others who receive the consultation services*. During the initial contact, expectations, responsibilities, and roles are often defined. Fortunately, considerable findings from research have been gathered that tell us how to be effective consultants. In this chapter we begin to share some of that information related to rapport development and how it can be put into practice.

PROFESSIONAL COMMUNICATION SKILLS

There are various *professional communication skills that can be used to help you in*:
- developing rapport with your consultees;
- gathering relevant information *for your client's functional assessment*; and
- involving the consultee in the goal and intervention selection process.

The first of these skills is called reflecting.

Reflecting

Reflecting, part of active listening, conveys to consultees that you have heard and understand what is being said. Although many of us use reflecting and many of the other active listening skills described in this chapter, we are often not aware of doing so. Here, we hope to alert you to their purposes and importance. Reflecting often serves three major important purposes: 1) it conveys to your consultees that you have heard and/or understand what has been said; 2) it prompts further elaboration; and 3) the consultee can correct any misperceptions that you might express during your reflection.

DEVELOPING RAPPORT & COLLABORATIVE RELATIONSHIPS • 17

REPEATING IN TOTAL. There are three methods of reflecting. One method involves repeating in total the statement that has been said. This method should seldom be used. If used frequently, particularly in a mechanical, impressionless manner, it can harm rapport, because your frequent parroting quickly becomes irritating. However, it can be helpful when your consultee's statement appears incongruous or surprising to you. Let's look at a home and a school example. (P = parent, T = teacher, M = manager and C = consultant.)

P: I'm about to kill Jimmy.
C: You're about to kill Jimmy?
P: Well, not really, but I'm so frustrated with the way he treats his sister, I just don't know what to do.

T: I just don't know what to do about Maria
C: You don't know what to do about Maria?
T: Yes! I've tried a variety of things and nothing seems to work.

M: I just don't think millennials are cut out to do manual labor.
C: You don't think millennials are cut out to do manual labor?
M: Well, it just seems like they don't want to really work and I don't know how to get them to want to work.

REPEATING THE LAST FEW WORDS. A second method of reflecting involves repeating, or mirroring, the last couple of spoken words by your consultee. This method is used to convey that you have heard what has been said and to prompt further elaboration. It can be used frequently, but again, do not over use it. You can intersperse it with comments such as "uh huh," "mmm," "Yes, I see," and head nods to convey that you are following what is being said. But, again, be careful not to overuse any of the expressions or head nods in that their habituation can be distracting to your consultees and interfere with rapport development. Here are some examples of repeating the last couple of words:

P: The trouble often starts while they are watching TV.
C: Watching TV?
P: Yes. They can't seem to agree on what to watch.
C: To watch?
P: Yes. They argue, and then Jimmy often becomes aggressive.

T: Maria is just all over the place.
C: All over the place?
T: Yes, she gets out of her seat, wonders around the class or just sits and stares out the window.

M: When I walk by Mark's station, he is constantly not working.
C: Not working?
M: Yes. He is usually on his iPhone.
C: On his iPhone?
M: Yes. He is texting or on social media, I think.

PARAPHRASING. Paraphrasing is the third method of reflecting. It is the most helpful of the three to convey your understanding and to help ensure you are not misinterpreting what the consultee has said. To paraphrase, simply *restate in your own words what the consultee has said.* Here are some examples:

P: I've been thinking that if Jimmy doesn't start treating his sister with more respect I might call my mom to see if he can stay there for awhile.
C: Sounds like you're feeling really frustrated and near the end of your patience.

T: If she doesn't start behaving I'm going to try to refer her to special education.
C: You seem really frustrated with Maria's behavior, and are about to call it quits in trying to get her to behave in your classroom because nothing seems to work.

M: I think if Mark doesn't start working and stop playing on his iPhone, I'm going to have to can him.
C: Seems like you are frustrated and need Mark to work when he is supposed to be working and only use his iPhone on his breaks.

Use paraphrasing, then, to communicate your respect and understanding of the situation. Do not rely on just your attention to convey your understanding.

Clarification

You will often need to seek clarification of what the consultee has said to better understand the situation. *Clarification helps you, the consultant, to more thoroughly understand what the consultee meant by a particular statement.* And, like reflection, clarification helps you to communicate active listening to your consultee. Also, it is very helpful in getting vague behavior statements by the consultee operationalized so that they are both observable and measurable. With clarification, *you convey your confusion and need for clarification.* Here are examples:

P: It's just his aggression I can't tolerate.
C: Aggression? Can you help me understand what he is doing when he is being aggressive?
P: Sure. He hits her and she leaves the room crying.

C: So your major concern is his hitting his sister. Is that right?
P: That *and* his yelling at her.

T: Yes, Maria continues to be all over the place no matter what I say or do.
C: So is what you want to see is Maria in her seat doing her math?
T: That's it! You hit the nail on the head.

M: He is always on his iPhone.
C: Always? How often do you go by Mark's work station and check to see if Mark is working or on his iPhone?
M: I check every two hours when I look to see how many welding projects he has finished.
C: When you check on the number of projects he has finished, is he usually behind?
M: Well... no, but he is on his iPhone.
C: So, would it be fair to say that you are not concerned with the amount of work Mark accomplishes, but rather that he is on his iPhone at inappropriate times?

Note above in the classroom illustration how the consultant used clarification to establish a behavior goal to work on. Also, when using clarification, be sure to obtain your consultee's confirmation regarding your assessment of what your consultee wants, or means, by his or her statements. By doing so, you find out if you are on the right track and have a complete picture of the issues (i.e., you find out if you understand or not). For example, in the above parent example, the consultant found out that the parent not only wanted the hitting to cease, but also the yelling. Asking for confirmation, then, is simply a helpful way to keep the channels of communication open, and lets you know if you understand what your consultee has been saying. So, when you are confused or not sure, seek clarification. Do not wait and hope the issue will eventually get clarified.

I-Statements

Generally, *it is best to minimize your use of direct questions.* A series of questions often are associated with the role of talking to an expert. We have all experienced going to see a doctor, car mechanic, a tax expert (perhaps a CPA), etc. They all ask a series of direct questions and then assume the responsibility for diagnosis and treatment. If they don't ask a particular question you thought they might, that probably means that it's not important, so you do not provide that information. Questions now and then can prove helpful, but a series of direct questions and answers can limit the information you obtain. They also often result in the consultee assuming you will determine what should be done and do it, resulting in their turning the client over to you to work with, rather than both of you (after all, that is what happens with the M.D., mechanic, CPA, and others who ask a series of questions). Instead you need the consultee to become an active partner in selecting goals and interventions. Eventually, the consultee will need to be prepared to assume total responsibility for program implementation.

So, you are probably asking by now, "If I minimize direct questions, how do I get enough information to help design an effective intervention?" An alternative to a series of direct questions, we find most helpful, is to share your need for additional information with your consultees, which helps to move you from the expert role to a collaborative, team relationship. You do this by beginning your statement with the word "I" or "'I'm." We used an I statement above while seeking clarification when we asked for help by communicating your state of confusion. Obviously not all questions need to start with "I," but it is most helpful to intersperse them among other questions to minimize or eliminate asking a series of direct questions. *Using I-statements helps involve your consultees and helps them to recognize their importance in goal selection and intervention.*

Here are some more examples of using I-statement to help you as you gather information about what might be prompting and reinforcing the occurrence of the youngster's behavior.

> "I think I've got a good grasp now of the behavior of concern, but I don't believe I have a clear understanding yet of just what might be all the situations that set the behavior off. Can you help me gain a better understanding of those situations?"

> "OK, I'm gaining a picture of what occurs prior to her yelling and hitting, but I don't have a clear picture of what happens, and who does what, after the behavior occurs other than his sister crying and leaving?"

> "I thought yelling and hitting were the major issues. But now I'm hearing that he also bites?"

Note how the I-statements above can help you to complete an A-B-C, or a contingency analysis, of the target behavior (A = antecedent stimuli related to the occurrence of the behavior; B = clarification and operationalization of the target behavior; and, C = the consequences related to the behavior's occurrence.)

Content and Affect Messages

As you gather information related to the client's behavior, you need to listen carefully to tell whether the consultee is conveying information or feelings. **Content messages** *provide information.* **Affect messages** *convey emotions or feelings.*

When consultees share an affect message about an inability to solve a problem, they often experience the risk of your disapproval and/or the disappointment of you not having heard their affect message. Also, affect messages tend to repeat themselves if they are not heard. Thus, it is important that you communicate that you have heard by paraphrasing the affect of your consultee's expression without disapproval. Similarly, when a content message occurs, do not try to reflect affect, but stay with content in your reflections. Here are some examples:

"I feel discouraged. Nothing seems to work."

This is an affect statement. you might respond with a paraphrase such as:

"Seems like you are really feeling down as a result of not being able to come up with an intervention that works."

"Yes, do you have any suggestions?"

Your consultee has now moved to content, so you need to reflect content:

"I have no magic solution, but let's sit down and brainstorm and see if we can't come up with some possible interventions that might work. OK?"

Note that in the example above, the collaborative approach to deciding what interventions to implement may have prevented the consultant from diminishing the consulate's previous attempts to manage the behavior by acting like the behavior can easily be changed by a quick recommendation.

It also is helpful to reflect in an A-B-C format whenever possible. For example, in response to an affect statement such as the following:

"The last time Maria was not doing her work I really felt discouraged because I prepared a special interesting assignment, to help her stay on task."

You might say:

So, when Maria was not on task (A), this left you discouraged (B), because you had gone to the trouble of coming up with a motivating assignment and it too failed (C).

Here, you state what triggered the feeling (A), what the feeling was (B), and the reason for the feeling (C).

Confrontation

In the initial contact with your consultees, it is not uncommon for the consultee to express negative feelings. It is helpful to address this affect before moving on to content. However, you need to be careful so that you don't find yourself serving as a therapist to the consultee. That is not your responsibility nor have you been trained as a psychological therapist. When it appears that the expression of affect is interfering with making progress in helping the client, you need to express your concern by confronting the consultee regarding the progress being made to help the client. For example, you might say something like:

"We have spent the past two meetings sorting out some of the frustrations that you have been experiencing with (Maria/Jimmy/Mark). My concern is that we have not yet begun to address what we might do help (Maria/Jimmy/Mark) to change her/his behavior. Without dealing with this issue, things will remain much the way they are currently. I wonder what you might want to do about this?"

Confrontation, then, *entails using an I-message to convey your awareness of a discrepancy between on-going events and earlier agreements or understanding. It also usually incorporates your feelings and the reason for your feelings.*

Confrontation has to be used carefully, in that it does have the potential to generate negative feelings. As a result, we would recommend that you do not use confrontation during your first two meetings with your consultees. After that, if you find that it is probably necessary to promote progress, be sure to incorporate the I-message when conveying your thoughts. Here are some more examples of possible confrontation statements:

"When you were late for today's meeting, I became frustrated in that I began to question whether you are committed to working together on this referral."

"I need to share some feelings I have regarding our last meeting."

"I would prefer not to meet in the faculty room in that the problem you have shared with me seems serious and I don't want to risk being interrupted."

"I don't think that 10 minutes will be enough time for us to meet, and hope we can find a time to meet for at least 30 minutes to get started. There is a lot of information I need from you to begin to understand this situation."

Summarizing

It is important to summarize your understanding periodically during your discussions with your consultee. Summarizing periodically serves to up-date you and the consultee as to what has been covered so far, and sets the stage for further progress. We have found it very useful to use when:

- The consultee starts repeating what was said previously.
- The consultant is beginning to feel overwhelmed with the amount of information being presented.
- You or the consultee aren't sure as to what has been covered or what to discuss next.
- You are ready to move onto a different topic.

DEVELOPING RAPPORT & COLLABORATIVE RELATIONSHIPS • 23

To summarize, you will often have to halt the interaction to share what you have heard up to a given point in your discussion with your consultees. Here is an example:

"Let's stop for a moment. I need to share what I think I've heard so far to make sure we are on the same track. First, when Maria is asked to do math, she looks out the window or wanders around the classroom. When this occurs you have asked her to sit down at her desk and do her work. Yet, she is soon out of her seat again or daydreaming. This extensive off-task behavior does not tend to occur in other situations. Is this correct so far?"

Notice how the summary was presented in an A-B-C format[1]. First you mention the antecedent (math assignment), then the behavior, and then the consequences to the behavior. By summarizing in this manner, you are able to begin to help your consultees learn how to do contingency analyses, or the beginning of a functional behavior assessment. This can help them analyze and determine possible reasons as to why specific behaviors may be occurring.

Here is another example:

"I need to stop to see if I'm understanding what you have been sharing with me so far. When watching TV during the evening with his sister, Jimmy often yells and hits his sister. You have disciplined him by taking away part of his allowance most every time the behavior occurs. At other times you have yelled at him to stop. Is this correct?"

Here is another example:

"Let me recap to make sure I'm following what you have been saying. When you go to check on the welders' progress on their assigned tasks at the two hour mark, you go down the line starting with Jake. After checking Jake's progress, you go to Mark's station to check his progress. And Mark is on his iPhone and you have to ask him to get off of it so you can check his progress? Then once you have checked his progress, you move on to the next work station, which is two feet from Mark's."

Non-Vocal Communication

A lot of our communication is communicated by what is typically referred to as non-verbal communication[2]. We mentioned head nods previously. Here are a

---

[1] For a more elaborate discussion of conducting functional assessments, including exercises in identifying the function of various behaviors, see Chapter 6 of *Principles of Applied Behavior Analysis for Behavior Technicians and Other Practitioners,* 2nd. Ed. (2019) by Wallace and Mayer.

[2] According to Skinner's description of verbal behavior, these forms of communication also are called verbal behavior, but most people call them non-verbal.

number of additional *suggestions* regarding non-spoken cues and note taking that we believe can help you communicate more effectively.

POSTURE. It is best to appear relaxed with an open posture, slightly leaning toward the consultee. People tend to mirror other's behavior, so the consultee may appear relaxed and open in return. Sit next to consultee at about a 90-degree angle with arms relaxed on your lap or chair, or one arm may be taking notes (see below). Do not appear stiff, with arms folded across your chest. This later posture promotes distance, and does not communicate a concerned, relaxed helpful individual.

FACIAL EXPRESSIONS. Achieve periodic eye contact to help convey your attending. Your facial expressions should be congruent with your words and feelings to present a model of honesty to support improved communication (e.g., furrowing your eyebrows and tilting your head while stating that you are confused). Facial expressions of questions, concern, or empathy can often better communicate these aspects of communication than words.

NOTE TAKING. Taking notes is a common practice. However, it can interfere with effective communication unless done correctly.

When taking notes, sit next to the consultee at about a 90-degree angle so the consultee can see what you are jotting down. If they do not see what you are jotting down, their anxiety is likely to increase and they will often wonder what it is you are writing about them, which can damage rapport.

It is important to *maintain eye contact during note-taking while the consultee is talking* to communicate interest. The lack of eye contact can be punishing to what the consultee is saying. This means that *you write only when you are speaking*, and you speak slowly and distinctly. When doing this, it is helpful to state a complete sentence, but write only the key words of the sentence. After all, it's only notes that you are taking. You are not writing a paper. As you write, you say what you are writing, so *the consultee can both see and hear what you are jotting down*.

Also, when taking notes, place them in an A-B-C format: You have three columns. Under the A column your notes state the setting and any antecedent events or objects that are related to the occurrence of the target behavior. The behavior identified that needs to be taught and/or changed (the target behavior) is operationalized in the B column. So, the B column is filled in first, followed by the A and C columns, which are filled in as events that precede and follow the target behavior are identified by the consultee. In the C column, as you probably guessed by now, you list consequences that appear related to the target behavior (who did or said what). As you continue to take notes in this fashion, the consultee is observing and hearing the A-B-C analysis that you are modeling for them. This can help them learn to analyze behavior. However, like many new behaviors, it does take time to become skilled at this type of note-taking, so we suggest you practice it with some of your friends and/or colleagues before using it with an actual consultee.

MULTICULTURALISM— DIVERSITY AND EQUITY IN CONSULTATION

It would be wrong for a book on consultation to not address how to consult from a multicultural perspective. Multiculturalism certainly can have an impact on developing rapport and developing collaborative relationships. However, it is only recently that behavior analysts have begun to seriously address multicultural practices (Fong et al., 2016; Zarcone, Brohead, & Tarbox, 2019). To address consultation from this perspective, it is important to understand what *multiculturalism* means.

Multiculturalism and Context

What is multiculturalism and how does one consult in a multicultural competent fashion? Moreover, how does the context in which one is consulting affect the process? These ideas and concepts are difficult for behavior analysts, but are cogent concepts that need to be addressed and included if one hopes to be an effective consultant and produce lasting behavior change. In consultation, multiculturalism is the way cultural diversity is included in the process of consultation itself. Awareness and understanding of cultural diversity and its impact on consultation, as well as the behavior change process, are necessary for effective consultation. We live in a multicultural world and diversity is all around (e.g., ethnic, gender, socio-economic status, sexual orientation differences, just to name a few). Historically, it has been suggested that to practice from a multicultural perspective, one must have cultural competence. However, more recently the term *competence* has been replaced by *humility* (Freshman, 2016; Wright, 2019). Competence implies that knowledge of every cultural variable can be acquired and then utilized in practice (the end goal); however, humility implies that we recognize our own cultural values, as well as how other cultures influence practice. Cultural humility requires an ongoing, lifelong learning course of action. It would be impossible to understand every cultural variable and how they may affect the consultation and behavior change process; however, it would be amiss to not include multicultural humility in a text on how to be an effective consultant.

The Association for Multicultural Counseling and Development offers a framework for incorporating multiculturalism into helping professions practices. One approach to implementing multiculturalism is the RESPECTFUL model (D'Andrea & Daniels, 2001). This model provides a framework for bringing awareness to the diversity of our clients, change agents, other professionals, and even what we bring to the table. Each letter in the word RESPECTFUL represents a different dimension to consider during your practice of behavior consultation. R = religion/spirituality; E = economic/social class background; S = sexual identity; P = personal style and education; E = ethnic/racial identity; C = chronological/lifespan status and challenges; T = trauma/crisis; F = family background and history; U = unique physical characteristics; and L = location of residence and language differences. As behavior analysts we know that such antecedents can affect the function of behavior by changing the value, or the effectiveness, of the consequences. Thus, we need to assess these different dimensions while we are assessing and working in diverse environments. In fact, one could argue that being aware of clients' and behavior change agents' multicultural backgrounds enables us to take those variables into account during our behavior change process. Moreover, it is imperative in effective consultation that we understand that *we, and all of our beliefs*, also affect the behavior change process. *A word of caution, though*: it is important to not look at the RESPECTFUL dimensions as just a list of *hot topics* to cover during the consultation process, but rather as potential variables that can affect the behavior change process (including consultation).

Being multicultural means considering the past history of these variables on behavior as well as their present influence on current contingencies. It is also important to understand the intersection of these variables and combined effects (Skinner, 1981).

Ethics of Multiculturalism

Besides being a good idea, including multiculturalism in our practice of ABA is required according to our *Professional and Ethical Compliance Code for Behavior Analysts* (BACB, 2017). In fact, 1.05 Professional and Scientific Relationships (c) explicitly states that: "differences in age, gender, race, culture, ethnicity, national origin, religion, sexual orientation, disability, language, or socioeconomic status" (p. 5) must be acknowledged when practicing ABA and that behavior analysts must be competent with how these variables affect their practice. Skinner describe these important variables as the third level of selection that occurs (Skinner, 1981). Thus, to practice within our seven dimensions of ABA we must incorporate them into our practice (Baer, Wolf, & Risley, 1968).

Incorporating Multiculturalism in Practice

Fong et al. (2016) provide some suggestions on how to apply cultural humility within practice. At the forefront of practicing from a multicultural perspective is to understand one's own "cultural values, preferences, characteristics, and circumstances" (p. 84) as well as those of one's clients. In fact, it is important to understand one's own cultural beliefs, the cultural beliefs of one's clients, and how they intersect and affect the relationship (in this case the consultation relationship). Awareness can lead to modifications of the intervention to account for these cultural influences resulting in more culturally appropriate models of service delivery. Incorporating multiculturalism in practice from a behavior analytic standpoint lacks clear and empirically demonstrated guidelines; however, it is possible to adopt methodology from other professions and apply them in a behavior analytic manner. Fong et al. suggest that the first step in cultural humility is to do a self-evaluation, or engage in an assessment of one's own cultural beliefs by engaging in a self-awareness process. To help with your self-evaluation, you might consider Leland and Stockwell (2019) self-assessment tool, with questions such as: "I do not knowingly engage in behavior that is harassing or demeaning to persons based on their gender identify, gender expression, or gendered preferences, interests, or behaviors" (p. 819). Or, within the RESPECTFUL model presented above, one would first identify oneself on each of the dimensions, identify the strengths and positives associated with each dimension, and then ask yourself how you might work with those who are different for each dimension.

For example, Mitch, who identifies himself as an atheist from an affluent upper-class socioeconomic status, gay, white male, from a two-parent family, and living in southern California, asks himself how these cultural variables will affect his consultation with Margaret, who identifies herself as a single-mother, practicing Catholic from a poverty socioeconomic status, heterosexual, Hispanic female, from a two-parent family, living in southern California. It is important for Mitch to take into consideration Margaret's beliefs when the two of them select the target behavior and context for Aiden's (her son) behavior plan. One of Margaret's self-disclosed struggles is taking Aiden to church and his engaging in problem behavior while Margret is receiving the eucharist. Without understanding how his own and Margret's religious beliefs influence what and how problem behavior should be targeted, the consultation process may break down and Margaret could generalize her lack of confidence to all behavior analysts.

Here are a couple of additional examples of how cultural values and/or beliefs can influence the effectiveness of consultation. Researchers (Zuckerman et al., 2017) have noted that Latino parents experience a significantly higher rate of trust issues than non-Latino White parents. Such mistrust might lead to diminished compliance, or treatment fidelity. As a second example, Dennison et al. (2019) have pointed out that a consultee who expects a warm informal discussion to occur prior to any discussion of a client's intervention, may find a violation of this cultural norm irritating. Such an outcome might damage the rapport that you have developed. Monitoring your consultee's nonvocal behaviors for signs of discomfort or displeasure might help you gain insight if this or other cultural norms have been violated. Always be sensitive to your consultee's non-vocal communication, and respect and value individual differences in relation to culture and values.

Sometimes respecting cultural values can conflict with your code of ethics. For example, should you respect the cultural value of your consultee giving you a gift to show their appreciation, or follow the BACB code of ethics by not accepting the gift? In plain English, there is no simple answer to this issue. Turning the gift down can damage the rapport that you have worked hard to establish (which we have experienced), but accepting it has the potential of tainting the professional relationship and putting your credential at risk. For now, we agree with Brodhead's (2019) position: "Any behavior analyst bound to the BACB Code must do his or her due diligence to minimize noncompliance with it, at the same time behavior analysts must do their due diligence to maintain respectfulness and appreciation for cultural values, as well as maintain actions that protect their credential" (p. 828).

The current literature on how to practice from within a multicultural perspective suggests that the best way to do so is to be aware of your own assumptions, values, and biases, as well as those of others. Ivey, Ivey, and Zalaquett (2018) and other books offer a number of reflective exercises to help you understand and communicate what your consultee is expressing. One way to understand multiculturalism is to reflect on situations you have personally encountered. They suggest reflecting on one's own experience with microaggressions, favoritism, and biases. By engaging in self-reflection and analyzing these types of interactions, one can elucidate how such variables affect relationships and potentially how they can affect the consultation process.

Beyond understanding one's own views and how others fall with respect to the different cultural dimensions, it is also important to understand that people may have different *worldviews*. Worldview, in short, is the way in which one interprets humanity and the world. It can also broadly describe one's way of viewing how things "work" in the world. As behavior analysts we view how the world works very differently than non-behaviorists. This difference, if you will, becomes extremely important when working within a team. As a behavior analyst consulting with a team, you might experience others who do not share your same worldview. It is important in these contexts not to be dogmatic. Understanding others' worldviews and not deeming them right or wrong will go a long way when consulting. For example, when one of the authors was consulting with a school district with respect to developing a behavior intervention plan for a young boy who engaged in aggression, understanding others' worldviews became very important to the success of the consultation and in the behavior change process for the young man. The school psychologist, administrator, and teacher thought the student engaged in aggression because of his home life (they included factors of socioeconomic status, race, parenting style, and parents' sexual identify as controlling factors).

Had I told them that their view of how the world worked was absurd and that the correct way was to only view the environmental relationship between stimuli, behavior, and consequence, I would have been fired on the spot. Instead of saying their worldview was wrong and mine was right, I acknowledge their worldview, but said for us to develop an effective behavior plan, we needed to look at the situation for a minute from a behaviorists' worldview. I showed them our worldview, by showing them that in a functional analysis I could increase or lower how much the student engaged in aggression. It wasn't a far jump to get them to see how incorporating a function-based intervention within their worldview framework, and developing an intervention, could change the student's behavior (which we did very successfully). Thus, the second step in practicing from a multicultural perspective is to understand that there is more than one way to view how the world works and that by simply rejecting other's views will not help you during the consultation process. Your job within the consultation process is *not* to change their worldview, but rather to change behavior. Thus, if you can merge worldviews for the sake of behavior change, job well done.

It also is important to realize that there are power imbalances (e.g., sexual identification and orientation, race, language, socioeconomic status, and representation) that "individuals and institutions must work to address through ongoing learning and self-reflection" (Wright, 2019, p. 805). For example, are minorities represented in decision making positions? Do factory line workers consist disproportionately of minorities, females, and lower socioeconomic level employees? Do special education classrooms consist disproportionately of minorities, male or females, and/or lower socioeconomic level students? Always look for and be aware of possible marginalization of communities.

ACTIONS TO AVOID

We suggest that you avoid the following common errors when working with consultees.

GIVING ADVICE. Many people attempt to give advice as a means of helping. However, when you sit down and discuss a case with a consulttee, that consultee has usually spent hours upon hours trying to teach or change a behavior, but has not been successful. If after conferring with the consultee for an hour or two, you advise them as to what they need to do, your consultee may feel that he or she must be very dense, or you, very gifted. Also, if the intervention is to be valued, you need to work out an intervention together that the two of you value and understand. Your consultee is much more likely to be committed to implementing the intervention with fidelity if involved in its development and selection. Plus, always realize that the consultee is probably more knowledgeable than you in knowing a variety of factors that can affect various interventions. The consultee has lived in that environment for years; you, only several hours.

ASKING A SERIES OF SPECIFIC QUESTIONS. We have addressed this issue earlier in this chapter. Briefly, it is best to work in a collaborative manner using the communication skills described above than asking a series of specific questions.

SHARING ONE OF YOUR SUCCESSES AS A MODEL TO IMITATE. Some consultants share a success with a client or two. However, this is not a good practice for the following reasons: It can appear that you are insecure and need to boast to enhance your status. It violates the principles of recognizing the uniqueness of each individual. Just because an intervention worked on another client, does not mean that it will work on your present client, nor does it mean that the consultee has the same skills and the previous one. (A factor you always need to consider when designing an intervention for the consultee to implement is the skill level of the consultee, and build on it as we will discuss in more detail in Chapters 4 & 6.) Sharing information about other client's successes may also promote unrealistic expectations or timelines for behavior change.

IGNORING THE CONSULTEE'S EXPRESSIONS OF CONCERN ABOUT BEING ABLE TO IMPLEMENT A PROGRAM, OR "ACCENTUATING THE POSITIVE." Some consultants attempt to encourage consultees to implement a program by giving them a pep talk stressing how competent they are, ignoring their expressed reservations to implementing a program. Such an approach does not acknowledge the consultees' feelings, leaving them feeling not understood, isolated, uncertain, and confused. Avoid pep talks, or accentuating the positive, and instead communicate your understanding, and jointly work out a program acceptable to both of you.

SUMMARY AND CONCLUSIONS[3]

A variety of professional communication skills have been shared in this chapter that we believe can improve: your information gathering during the initial interviews; establishing a safe environment for consultees discussing concerns; and, discussions concerning interventions. They help to promote rapport, gathering information for the client's functional assessment, and promote joint goal selec-

---

[3]Many of the communication skills described in this chapter are based on those used in counseling. For additional information and practice activities for using these skills, we believe that some excellent sources include an early book by E. H. Porter (1950), a book by Cormier & Cormier (1979), and the book by Ivey et al., 2018.

tion. In other words, they promote a collaborative relationship critical to effective consultation. However, be careful to not over-use the same communication skill. Overly frequent repetition of any communication skill can become distracting and interfere with rapport development.

In addition, multiculturalism certainly can have an impact on developing rapport and developing collaborative relationships. It is imperative that your consulting approach is sensitive to culture, diversity, and equity throughout the consultation process. It is not just about filling a quota of racially diverse employees. Nor is it just about equal pay for employees, regardless of their gender. Instead, "multiculturalism, diversity, and equity are about adopting and practicing a mind-set, a values-driven and data-guide process to employ and improve upon each and every day" (Zarcone, Brodhead, & Tarbox, 2019, p. 742). We are not talking about a one shot that ends the process. It is something you must re-investigate on a routine basis and with every new client, consultation project, or opportunity. It is important to use some of the tools we already have within our tool kit to help accomplish a multicultural approach (e.g., functional analyses, preference assessments). We also can do informal cultural, equity, and social validity assessments throughout the consultation process.

As you know, in addition to conducting interviews, part of doing an assessment of a client's behavior involves direct observation to help you determine what contingencies may be influencing the clients' behavior. When doing your interviews and observations, you will want to consider if any of your client's behaviors indicate a possible underlying medical condition. The next chapter, Chapter 3, is designed to help you identify behaviors during your observation and interviews that might indicate if your client should be referred for a medical assessment to determine if an underlying medical condition exists, and if a medical intervention is necessary. *Such a determination should be made for your client prior to and during baseline data collection.*

ACTIVITIES

1. Practice using reflecting and clarification with parent, teacher or supervisor (if such people are not available to you, use a friend). Ask the consultee to discuss what their child, student or employee (or if you are involving a friend, a relative, or close associate) do that they like and what behavior(s) they would like to stop or reduce. As you use reflecting and clarification, discover and obtain operational statements of at least one problem and goal behavior. Also, be sure to correctly reflect affect and content messages while using these skills with your con-

sultee. Do this activity with several people until your use of these communication skills begin to occur naturally.

2. Once you are comfortable with reflecting and clarification, review and use I-statements and summarization with your use of reflecting and clarification as you begin to conduct an A-B-C assessment of the problem and goal with your consultees. Again, practice this activity with your consultees until the combined use of reflecting, clarification, I-statements, and summarization begin to occur naturally for you.

3. Integrate confrontation (if needed) and the non-verbal skills, including note-taking, with the communication skills you have used in activities 1 & 2 while not using the "actions to avoid." This activity works best if you pair up with another student and provide vocal feedback to one another, or, if it is difficult to observe one another, video the activity and have your fellow student provide feedback (some instructors may want to see the video in which you integrate these skills, give you feedback, and/or use it as part of your class grade).

4. Do a RESPECTFUL assessment with yourself and/or a friend.

Chapter 3

Interfacing and Consulting with the Medical Profession

Linda Copeland MD, BCBA
One Community Health Center, Sacramento CA

Greg Buch Ph.D., BCBA-D
Pacific Autism Learning Services, Sacramento CA

Before you start deciding what interventions to use with dependent clients, and while you establish rapport and determine what behavioral issues need addressing, you also need to review the client's medical history, medications, and determine if medical clearance or a referral is necessary. This chapter addresses such issues and will help you recognize the existence of possible medical origins, if any, of the client's behavioral issues.

Behavior analysts are aware that they are ethically required to consult with medical professionals when treating behavioral conditions which may be influenced by medical or biological factors (Behavior Analysis Certification Board, 2014). Also, task F-1 of the BACB certification task list stipulates that you must review records and available data (including medical) at the onset of the case. However, knowledge regarding the potential benefits for clients that can be derived from ongoing coordination of care between medical and behavioral professionals still represents an emerging skill set for both medical and behavioral professionals. In this chapter, we will use brief case examples to illustrate the importance and value of: a) evaluating a client's medical history before providing consultation through record reviews and indirect assessments; b) recognizing behaviors and data patterns that may indicate medical origins of behavioral issues; c) using behavioral strategies to teach skills that facilitate clients' access to medical care; and d) providing direct behavioral consultation during medical care.

MEDICAL HISTORY AT INTAKE

Marcus

A behavior analyst was asked by the special education director of a school district to provide consultation for Marcus, a third grader in a regular-education classroom. The director reported that Marcus had been diagnosed with ADHD and was currently medicated for it (the school nurse administered a pill each morning). Marcus' main behavioral issues were reported to be difficulty staying on task and high levels of inappropriate spoken behavior with peers when he was supposed to be working.

The analyst requested Marcus' medical records from the school district and family. The district provided a psycho-educational report from a previous school district, which indicated: a) Marcus reported hearing voices in his head which told him to do things; and b) a nonspecific history of aggressive and hyperactive behaviors that the assessor suggested were the result of undefined prior traumatic experiences. Marcus' family also reported that he had been physically abused by a family member who was no longer present in the home. The family was unable to provide any documentation regarding Marcus' diagnostic history and did not know: a) the name of the physician who prescribed Marcus' current medication, or b) what the medication was. However, the family reported that they believed Marcus had been diagnosed with ADHD and that the medication he was taking was to help him stay focused.

With the family's permission, the analyst checked Marcus' medication bottle and found that he was currently taking fluoxetine, a medication for depression, sold under the brand name Prozac. The behavior analyst then found the prescribing physician by contacting Marcus' insurance plan. The prescribing physician reported that she had diagnosed Marcus with Disruptive Mood Dysregulation Disorder. The prescribing physician also reported that she had determined that prior reports of Marcus "hearing voices" had been mischaracterizations of negative self-talk, rather than evidence of hallucinations. The analyst and the physician coordinated care on the case and determined that behavioral support, in the form of antecedent modifications and a reinforcement system for on-task behavior, would be appropriate.

Marcus' case illustrates both the necessity of obtaining an accurate medical history before developing an intervention in collaboration with the school team, and the challenge that analysts often face in obtaining these histories, particularly when working in homes and educational settings. The behavior analyst's initial concern upon learning that the client reported hearing voices (a symptom of schizophrenia), was that the client's needs were outside her area of education and experience. However, the analyst recognized that it would also be inappropriate to reject the client on what appeared to be an incomplete and discrepant medical history.

Before serving a client, through consultation with the behavior change agent, behavior analysts should review: the client's medical history (including any and all psychiatric diagnoses); medications and their possible side effects (side effects can be discovered by going on the internet and asking, "What are the side effect of ___."); and any physiological or physical barriers to treatment (e.g., allergies, swallowing difficulties, motor disabilities such as lack of ambulation, etc.). Behavior analysts should confirm that their education and experience is consistent with the requirements of the case (in terms of diagnostic category and behavioral severity) and determine if the client's behaviors might need medical clearance before intervention. There are a number of clinical situations that often require in-depth medical evaluation and clearance in addition to good coordination of care. Top among these are severe self-injury (Iwata et al., 1994), severe psychiatric conditions (Newhouse-Oisten et al., 2017) and pediatric feeding disorders (Piazza, 2008). If a client does not have a clear diagnostic history, a thorough medical evaluation is indicated prior to developing intervention during consultation.

A complete medical history should include the following components (Copeland & Buch, 2019):

- Medical diagnoses
- Current medications, vitamins, supplements, dosages, and routes of administration
- All therapies that the client is receiving
- Contact information (name, phone number) of the primary care physician, dentist and any specialists
- Contact information and coordination of care permission forms (e.g., the "Authorization for release of patient information" form from the California Department of Health Care Services, 2013)
- Significant changes in diet, health status, medications, vitamins, or supplements
- Dates of last hearing and vision tests
- Surgeries
- Immunization record
- History of significant injuries and illnesses
- Medical restrictions such as diet or activities and any allergies to medicines, foods or other substances

- History of substance abuse
- Risks to self or others
- Department of Corrections supervision or court-ordered mental health or chemical dependency treatment

Any significant discrepancies or omissions in the medical record should be investigated before behavioral consultation is provided. Critical issues to watch out for include: a) lack of documentation for reported disorders; b) severe behaviors or conditions which appear to be unrecognized or untreated; and c) inaccurate or incomplete clinical information provided by caregivers or professional service providers.

THE POSSIBLE IMPACT OF MEDICAL CONDITIONS

During Behavioral Consultation

In a comprehensive behavioral approach, a behavior analyst should consistently look at the possibility that biological variables may be influencing behavior.

Steven

A practicing developmental pediatrician training for the BCBA credential was interning at a center-based therapeutic preschool run by behavior analysts. The pediatrician was assigned to conduct a functional behavioral assessment for Steven, a toddler who demonstrated a range of noncompliant and tantrum behaviors. Steven was reported to be in good health and took no medications. Direct observations indicated that, in addition to some clear noncompliant behavior (such as direct refusals), Steven had instances of falling to the ground. He appeared to suddenly lose all muscle tone, and then would collapse to the ground in an uncontrolled fashion. He would then get back up and seem fine, but appeared to be a little confused. Typically, children who engage in noncompliance or tantrums by throwing themselves to the ground voluntarily do so in a controlled fashion such that they are unlikely to get hurt in the process. The red flag in Steven's case was that he made absolutely no attempts to break or control his falls. The pediatrician knew from her medical training that his falling spells could represent a form of seizure called drop-attack seizures. This issue was discussed with his parents, who had never previously suspected that Steven might be having seizures. Steven was then promptly evaluated by a neurologist. An EEG confirmed the presence of drop-attack seizures, and they were successfully treated. Once medically stabilized, Steven made good progress in his ABA preschool program.

Many physiological conditions can negatively impact a client's behaviors and their responsiveness to intervention. At the obvious, and relatively mild end of the spectrum, is the common cold. Head colds often function as a motivating operation (MO) that can contribute to kids becoming grumpy and uncooperative. Behavioral support personnel can see when clients have colds and can either cancel or modify therapy accordingly. It is not necessary to develop behavioral interventions to address temporary increases in tantrums that occur as functions of such things as minor head colds. However, there are many other medical conditions (such as certain types of seizures) which significantly affect clients' behaviors. Some of these medical conditions can be essentially invisible to the observer. When a medical problem is not easily observable it is referred to as an occult condition. "Occult" medical conditions can remain undiagnosed and untreated for months or years, and behavior analysts may inadvertently collaborate with a team to treat their behavioral side effects if they remain unrecognized.

BEHAVIORS INDICATING POSSIBLE MEDICAL CONDITIONS

Behavior analysts are not trained to recognize medical or psychiatric conditions. However, there are some observable behaviors and data patterns which may indicate that a client is experiencing a medical condition (whether observable or occult) and that a medical referral and consultation would be appropriate. The following are some useful red flags for medical conditions which may impact client behavior, which should be addressed during consultation:

Red Flag	Possible Causes
Rapid, unusual weight gain or loss	psychiatric conditions like depression, or gastrointestinal, endocrine, or some other medical disorder
Loss of interest in most preferred foods & activities	depression; low thyroid hormone, GI issues, chronic illness
Areas of redness, swelling, or discoloration	indication of injury, pain and discomfort; allergic reaction
Labored breathing, sweating, looking extremely pale	possible indication of pain, respiratory problem such as asthma or serious infection like pneumonia, or an allergic reaction
Cyclical vomiting (vomiting that occurs in a predictable pattern across specific numbers of days or weeks)	neurological condition (Levinthal, 2016)

Red Flag	Possible Causes
Chronic poor focus, short attention span, distractibility, & impulsivity	Attention Deficit Hyperactivity Disorder
Wincing, moaning, doubled-over, back arching, grabbing or rubbing a body part, increased self-injurious new or relapsing behavior (SIB) with no change in the environmental antecedents or consequences	Indication of injury, pain and discomfort
Atypical inattention; repetitive eye-blinking and lip-smacking; twitching; and loss of postural tone	Seizure Disorder
Unusual difficulty in toilet training	GI or urinary conditions
Swallowing problems, bloating, cramping, nausea, vomiting, diarrhea	gastrointestinal disorder, certain types of infection (e.g. lower lobe pneumonia)
Cyclical patterns in maladaptive behaviors, including vomiting	Intellectually disabled women may have painful menses, known as dysmenorrhea, and can show self-injurious behavior in response to this (Taylor, Rush, Hetrick & Sandman, 1993)
Change in mood, mental status, habits, irritability, worry and avoidance, extreme anger, marked distractibility or hyperactivity, hearing voices	psychiatric disorders including mood disorders, schizophrenia, anxiety disorders, bi-polar disorder
Problems with sleeping and level or alertness and focus	possible sleep disorder, medication side effect, substance abuse issue, or neurological problem
Sudden changes in intensity, frequency or conditional probability of behavior or sudden emergence of a new problem behavior in the absence of changes in S^Ds, S^Rs & MOs	Multiple occult conditions
Gradual loss of motor skills: for instance, gait problems and loss of hand function	Rett Syndrome (Lane, Lee, Smith, Cheng, Percy & Glaze et al, 2011) or other neurodegenerative disorder
Decreases in compliance with verbal directions	Have been found to be related to hearing loss (Koffler, Ushakov, & Avraham, 2015)
Distinct changes in the function of a problem behavior	Client may be responding to internal cues such as pain, discomfort, anxiety and so forth; cues may come and go
Undifferentiated behavioral function	Again, client may be responding to internal cues.

Red Flag	Possible Causes
Rapid loss of cognitive or verbal skills:	May be found to be related to strokes, seizures, or severe mental health conditions such as psychosis, major depression and catatonia (Lisabethe, Brown, Hughes, Majersik, & Morgenstern, 2009). Loss of verbal comprehension and expression together with a severely abnormal EEG is associated with Landau Kleffner seizure syndrome (Chez, 2008)
Decreased level of awareness: mutism, staring, posturing, part of the body or the whole person freezing motionless in place, frozen grimaces, possible associated incontinence	Neurological or psychiatric condition such as selective mutism (anxiety-related), seizure, or catatonia
Falling to the ground with no attempt of person to break their fall	Drop-attack seizures
Severe behaviors related to avoidance of specific stimuli or circumstances	Panic attacks, post-traumatic stress symptoms, victim of abuse, other
Strict adherence to a highly repetitive routine	Possible obsessive compulsive disorder (OCD), anxiety

DETERMINING BEHAVIOR'S COMMUNICATIVE INTENT WITH CLIENTS WHO HAVE LIMITED SPEAKING SKILLS

Clients with limited talking skills often cannot describe their symptoms or verbally express their pain or discomfort. As with an infant who is crying, you need to determine what is being communicated by the client's behavior. Here are some examples:

- Disruptive outbursts by a client occurred in school and at home. A scatter plot revealed that this disruptive behavior only occurred in rooms that had old, rapidly flickering fluorescent lights. A neurological workup combined with changing the lighting (the strobe effect was a trigger for occult seizures) solved the problem.
- A client's SIB only occurred when a radio was playing. It was found that each time such episodic SIB occurred, the client was experiencing onset of a recurrent ear infection. When the infection was cleared with antibiotics, the radio playing no longer bothered the client (O'Reilly, 1997).
- A teen girl with Autism Spectrum Disorder (ASD)-level 3 severity, began to hit her eyes. An eye exam performed several years before had been nor-

mal. A repeat eye exam showed rapid development of bilateral cataracts blocking her vision. After successful cataract surgery, eye-hitting ceased.

- A client with intellectual disability and limited talking skills began to pound his forehead against walls. A dental exam revealed a dental abscess that, when treated, resulted in resolution of the head-banging (note: hitting or banging one's head may be attention-seeking, escape-related or could relate to internal pain cues such as from migraine headache, sinus infection, or toothache).
- A young man with ASD (level 2 severity) started having transition problems from a preferred computer activity to an outdoor activity (transitioning to outside was not a previous problem). A functional assessment showed a clear avoidance function for going outside on bright sunny days, but not during twilight hours. An eye doctor discovered that the man had glaucoma (sunlight causes eye pain in glaucoma).

MAKING THE MEDICAL REFERRAL

Medical referrals should only be made after appropriate consent has been granted by a parent or legal guardian. Once consent is obtained, it is usually best not to depend solely on parents or legal guardians to make the referral. They may not be able to communicate the behavior analyst's concerns clearly or be able to communicate the clinical rationale for seeking a medical evaluation. Analysts may provide medical personnel with information on the magnitude and significance of any change in the client's level of functioning, as well as on the significance of specific behavioral data collected. Some medical personnel find the following information to be an aid with regard both to diagnosis and to assessing medical treatment efficacy:

- Clearly defined target behaviors
- Graphs of the duration or rate of occurrence of target behavior(s) plus ABC (Antecedent, Behavior, Consequence) information
- Scatter plot data indicating in what situation the behavior tends to occur

OTHER AREAS BEHAVIOR SPECIALISTS MIGHT CONSULT REGARDING MEDICAL CONDITIONS

Behavior specialists can make invaluable contributions to the overall medical care of their clients in a broad range of clinical situations. The following suggestions highlight the wide scope of potential assistance behavior specialists can offer. They include data collection that can facilitate collaborating and various medical-related areas in need of possible behavioral consulting:

- Collecting and graphing data on possible medication side effects as well as the intended effects of medications on target behaviors
- Teaching clients to remain immobile during imaging studies
- Teaching clients increased health-related self-management skills such as how to use a glucose monitoring device for blood sugar tests (Heinicke & Carr, 2014; LeBlanc, Heinicke, & Baker, 2012), how to use a peak flow meter to monitor breathing, how to take pills or other forms of medications (McComas, Wacker, & Cooper, 1998) and how to document the results, if needed.
- Teaching clients to wear hearing aids or glasses (Deleon, Hagopian, Rodriques-Catter, Bowman, Long, & Boelter, 2008)
- Helping clients learn to tolerate wearing a prosthesis (Richling, Rapp, Carroll, Smith, Nystedt, & Siewert, 2011).
- Helping clients tolerate injections, dental exams, and dental procedures (Allen & Wallace, 2013)

As of the writing of this chapter it is unfortunate that most medical professionals are still unfamiliar with behavior analysis as a field. Consequently, it is currently up to behavior analysts to initiate coordination of care for mutual clients with medical staff.

A CLOSER LOOK AT CONSULTATION: MULTIDISCIPLINARY EXAMPLES

Case 1

A behavior analyst received a referral to collaborate with a mother of a young man with developmental disabilities on his refusal to wear prescribed leg splints. He would engage in physical aggression toward his mother if she prompted him to wear the devices. Immediately upon meeting the young man and his mother, it was apparent that a medical consultation with the doctor that prescribed the splints was necessary. Thus, as part of the initial assessment, the BCBA met with the doctor, the client, and the mother. There was a several-fold need for this medical consultation: in part to ensure proper fit of the leg splints, to obtain a clear idea of how to wear the splints, to know when and for how long per day that the client was required to wear them and to clarify the long-term benefits of wearing the splints. Based on the consultation, it was discovered that the splints had not been adjusted as the young man had grown. The mother was trying to get her son to wear splints that were too small and extremely aversive. New splints were ordered prior to beginning the behavioral intervention. After the new splints were made, a behavioral intervention was implemented to teach the client to wear his leg splints and decrease his aggressive outbursts. The intervention included a shaping program (to increase the duration the client wore the splints per day), a behavioral contract (indicating the reinforcers the client would receive for wearing the splints), and a self-management program to relieve the mother from having to be the one to prompt the client to wear his splints. The young man not only started wearing the splints, but he managed his own behavior and stopped arguing with his mother. At follow-up visits with the doctor, the BCBA was able to share the data regarding the young man's wearing of his splints (days worn and for how long). In the end, after wearing the corrective splints for eight hours per day for many months, the young man was able to correct his orthopedic issue and the splints were discontinued by the medical doctor.

Case 2

A young adult man with developmental disability required relatively simple abdominal surgery related to a digestive tract problem. He had to eat nothing by mouth for a time both prior to and after the surgery, so he was given fluids intravenously. Fortunately, the surgery was quite successful without any immediate apparent complications. All of his vital signs showed that he was recovering nicely from the surgery. The young man was an orphan who had only recently been placed in a residential care home with no family and with totally new care providers who did not know him well. He was reported to be "nonverbal," making communication challenging. By clinical policy, the man could not be discharged from the hospital after abdominal surgery until he successfully resumed eating meals by mouth. When it came time to offer him regular food again, to the surprise of all the medical staff, he refused to eat. Instead, he curled into a ball in his bed. He would only drink water. This went on for days, to the point where he started to lose weight. Medical tests and abdominal imaging studies were done to make sure there was no complication from surgery. None were found. One of his doctors then ordered that a tube be placed through his nose and into his stomach, to see if his stomach could tolerate liquid food. The nursing staff did not know how to explain the tube placement to the patient, and the procedure was quite aversive to him. He fought having the tube and many times succeeded in pulling the tube out. For the next several days, liquid food was forced into his stomach in this manner. Physically he seemed to tolerate the liquid food, but he persistently fought the feedings. It became progressively more difficult to even try to place the feeding tube. The young man withdrew further, spending his days curled in a ball and growing weaker. A psychiatrist was then consulted by the medical team. Consideration was given as to whether the young man was showing signs of serious clinical depression. However, before formally diagnosing him with depression and starting treatment for this, a decision was made to consult with a BCBA first. The behavior analyst reviewed the patient's medical history and talked with the residential home care providers and with medical staff. Upon completing this review, the BCBA conducted a preference assessment at a level the young man could understand. The BCBA held up a clearly visible Snicker's candy bar in one hand (a known powerful reinforcer for the patient) and a plate of hospital food in the other hand. Upon seeing the Snicker's bar, the young man's eyes lit up and he made a clear, eager pointing gesture toward the Snicker's bar, which when offered he consumed with pleasure. The BCBA assisted the medical staff in creating a simple picture choice board with menu items and pictures of other basic needs and activities, to give the patient a method for functional communication. His residential care home staff brought in home-cooked meals (which he clearly preferred over hospital food). He regained his lost weight, improved his strength and was soon able to be discharged from the hospital.

Case 3

A woman with Down Syndrome in her twenties needed surgery for progressing cataracts in both eyes. She had a history of often picking at her face, at skin sores, bandages, and wounds, making it very difficult to leave bandages in place or to allow wounds to heal. To minimize the number of times she was exposed to anesthesia and for a variety of other reasons, it was felt best to complete both cataract surgeries at the same time. However, there was great concern that she would likely try to pick at her face and eyes after the surgery, which could disrupt the delicate sutures in her healing eyes. She was a client at a developmental regional center, which called together a multidisciplinary team to meet with the client, family and medical staff to create a strategy for how best to manage her post-operative care. Because it would be hard to manage bandaging both eyes at one time, and the presence of bandages would also likely prompt the picking, another means of protecting her eyes during the healing phase was needed. The protection needed to be something the client could not remove on her own, as she was prone to do. The BCBA and the occupational therapist on the team brainstormed together and came up with a solution. She was fitted for a fencing mask that covered her whole face but allowed her to see. The advantage of the fencing mask is that it latches in the back, which made it difficult for her to reach and remove. Additionally, her family shared she had shown a recent interest in a simple crocheting task. The BCBA and Occupational Therapist (OT) set up a teaching program for her to effectively learn this task through shaping and chaining, which proved greatly reinforcing for her and kept her occupied for substantial amounts of time (the crocheting activity was differentially incompatible with picking at her face and eyes). She successfully and promptly healed after her double eye surgery.

Case 4

A 16-year-old young man diagnosed with autism attended both regular and special education classes at his local high school, and his conversational skills were an area of relative strength. He was able to maintain conversations on favored topics, such as horror movies and cars, for ive to ten minutes. Eric's family consulted a behavior analyst with concerns regarding noncompliance, tantrums, and aggression. Eric required multiple spoken and physical prompts to bathe himself, brush his teeth, get dressed, and leave the house. Compliance with these demands had been an issue since preschool. However, over the previous year, Eric's resistance to demands had escalated. He would repeatedly argue and scream when instructed to get dressed and would punch and wrestle with his parents when prompted to leave the house. Neighbors had called child protective services multiple times and Eric was missing two to three days of school per week. The behavior analyst observed Eric's morning routine before school, and on the weekend before going to a movie (a preferred activity). The tantrums and aggression occurred both days, but rapidly subsided once Eric was in the car. The behavior analyst noted that on both days, Eric opened and closed his car door repeatedly before getting in. When queried, Eric's mother reported that this occurred every time Eric got in the family car, and that Eric had to do it exactly 25 times. When asked, Eric confirmed that he needed to open and close the door exactly 25 times, but he could not explain why. The behavior analyst recognized that this behavior was possibly consistent with obsessive compulsive disorder (OCD) and referred the family for a psychiatric evaluation. Eric was diagnosed with OCD and medicated with the SSRI medication Zoloft. Following medication for two months, Eric's tantrums, aggression, and repetitive behaviors had subsided. The behavior analyst subsequently provided behavioral interventions to address deficits in executive functioning and pragmatic social skills.

SUMMARY AND CONCLUSIONS

Practice behavior analysis wisely, keeping Code 3.02 of the Professional Ethical Compliance Code for Behavior Analysts ever in mind. Obtain medical consultation first if there is any serious consideration that behaviors of targeted interest may be controlled by biological variables. Recognize that your skills can often be best utilized when there is coordination of care for clients, behaviorally and medically. Because of your specialized training and observational skills, you are in an optimal position to help highlight when there might be medical causes for maladaptive behaviors. Similarly, you may be the first or only healthcare professional to recognize the potential presence of occult medical conditions and thereby recommend necessary medical consultation. This is especially true for clients with communication problems. By employing strategies to effectively interface with medical professionals, you can reduce the probability of inappropriate behavioral interventions for medical problems and medical professionals will in turn become more accustomed and familiar with behavior analysis. Additionally, by continued outreach to the medical community through offering your services to teach clients health-related skills, you can increase client access to timely medical assessments and treatment and can also increase their ability to self-manage their health care needs.

ACTIVITIES

1. Look up the possible side effects of a medication that you or an acquaintance is using and list them.
2. Review the red flags indicating possible medical conditions and describe why it is important to be familiar with them.
3. Give examples of the possible communication intent of at least three non-vocal behaviors.
4. List what information you should provide when making a medical referral.

Chapter 4

Promoting Implementation with Fidelity

We emphasized the use of professional communication skills and observable behaviors that might indicate a medical condition in the previous two chapters. As mentioned, communication skills help you establish rapport and help you to jointly identify goals and possible intervention strategies. You will need to continue to use these skills throughout your consultation contacts as you modify and select goals and interventions and as you monitor the implementation and success of those interventions. However, as pointed out in Chapter 3, before program implementation, you also need to obtain medical consultation prior to intervention whenever it appears that possible biological variables may be influencing your client's behavior.

Assuming you have a green light to proceed, in this chapter we emphasize strategies that you can use to help consultees start implementing the intervention(s). We start by presenting and discussing resistance and various concerns that some consultees have about aspects of using behavioral programs, followed by a discussion of various prompting strategies. We end by pointing out the importance that contextual fit has on any intervention you might consider. All of these topics can influence the degree to which selected programs are implemented with accuracy or fidelity by your consultees.

ADDRESS RESISTANCE TO IMPLEMENTING THE INTERVENTION

When consulting, you are occasionally likely to come across resistance from a consultee. In fact, although resistance is difficult to understand and is frustrating, it is not uncommon. It is likely to occur when the consultee is not the one seeking consultation per se. The key to understanding and dealing with resistance is to understand *why* it occurs and to not take it as a personal reflection of your consultation abilities. If we look at the resistance from a behavior analytic point of view, it makes sense that it occurs. If we are asking the consultee to engage in a new behavior, maybe the response is not in the person's repertoire and needs to be trained. If the behavior is in the person's repertoire, but they still aren't engaging in the behavior, it is likely that the behavior is not producing reinforcement while the old way of behaving is being reinforced. Thus, we need to set up a behavior plan to teach the new behavior or use differential reinforcement to reinforce the new behavior and not the old behavior (just like we do for our clients).

Understanding Resistance

The first thing one must do when faced with resistance from the consultee is to support the consultee's expression of resistance (do NOT become defensive), and you are not there to spy on them or to report bad data to their supervisor. To be effective as a consultant, you must create a situation for the consultee in which it is safe for them to reveal anxiety-provoking information and obstacles to follow through (Schein, 1999). This is also a great time to use some soft skills such as empathy (e.g., statements of understanding related to the resistance, or paraphrasing what you believe the consultee is experiencing based on their behavior). Use your developing rapport and collaborative relationship skills (Chapter 2) to understand the function of the resistance behavior. Put your behavior analytic lens on to analyze the resistance (i.e., treat the resistance as an operant). Is the consultee resistant because they lack the skills necessary to engage in the behavior you are asking them to do; does the environment support old ways vs. new ways of behaving; or, is your presence viewed as aversive vs. helpful? These are the environmental situations you must assess to replace resistance with acceptance and collaboration. Just like doing a skill assessment before teaching a new behavior to clients and doing a functional behavior assessment before eliminating an unwanted behavior, it is important to assess the situation when dealing with resistance from a consultee. Once you understand the *why* behind the resistance, you can use your behavior analytic skills to overcome the resistance.

Overcoming Resistance

If after you discover from your analysis of the environment supporting the resistance that indeed the resistance is related to a skill deficit, use **Behavior Skills Training** (elaborated upon starting on page 56) to teach the skill to the consultee. Even if you have already done competency-based training, the environment may be different enough from the training environment that the consultee needs more training on how to behave in that specific situation. If you have thinned the reinforcement schedule for the behavior, increase the reinforcement schedule and thin slower. Use functional reinforcers rather than arbitrary reinforcers (remember, sometimes using negative reinforcement, such as allowing them to vent or take a break contingent on them engaging in the behavior) to reinforce the new behavior. Also, be sure you have addressed your consultee's concerns (see below), and save your attention for when they engage in the behavior you want vs the behavior you don't. Remind yourself, *they are not engaging in resistance to get to you, they are engaging in it because it is being reinforced.* For example, if the function of a client's yelling behavior is to gain attention, she will likely cease yelling behavior if her mother reprimands her for yelling. Thus, her mother is negatively reinforced (the yelling stops) for providing the client with attention that is contingent on yelling. We must use behavior analytic procedures to overcome their resistance. It is always a good idea at the beginning of any consultation relationship to make yourself a reinforcer! Remember a little noncontingent reinforcement goes a long way in creating a positive relationship and avoiding resistance in the first place.

Addressing Concerns

You will find that some of your consultees will express one or more of the following concerns. It is important that you *address any concern that they may express.* The following concerns, if not addressed, often result in resistance as shown by poor program implementation. Here are some common concerns that you must address if you find your consultee is experiencing one or more of them.

EXPERIENCING DISCOMFORT. "I feel awkward using praise and acknowledging good behavior. It seems artificial." One response you can provide is that this is not at all unusual. We all feel a bit ill at ease the first several times we attempt a new skill. Recall the first time you tried to learn to swim, dance, golf, etc. However, after practice and reinforcing feedback for your successes, you gradually began to feel comfortable at the activities, even liking some of them. Using behavioral methods, such as praising appropriate behavior, usually produces its own reinforcers in the form of improved positive reactions from the recipients. Eventually, you will even find yourself enjoying the process.

FINDING THE TIME. "This sounds awfully time consuming. I don't think I have the time to do this." In response, first, of course, make sure you are not trying to get the consultee to do too much at the beginning of program implementation. Be sure to start with achievable goals and procedures that are simple for the consultee, and as mentioned near the end of Chapter 2, communicate your understanding and jointly work out a program acceptable to you both. Also, point out: 1) the amount of time they are currently investing in addressing the unacceptable behavior(s); 2) how their time invested up-front will pay off as the problem begins to diminish and the interpersonal relationship improves; and 3) the more they practice the skill, the more natural it will become and take hardly any time or effort.

USING BRIBERY. "Isn't this a form of bribery?" No! Bribery has no place in our interventions. Bribery is used primarily for the benefit of the person who delivers it, instead of for the recipient as in the behavioral approach. The aim of bribery is to corrupt, conduct or pervert judgment, or to promote dishonest or immoral behavior. Bribes are often presented before the act (i.e., used as a carrot), whereas reinforcement can only happen afterward.

Related to bribery concerns is the notion of "paying" or having to positively recognize others for behaving properly. "They should *want* to do this. I shouldn't have to bribe them." The fact is, individuals may not want to do what they should do. And, why do we expect others to engage in behavior that does not produce a reinforcing outcome for that behavior? Would you work at your job if you did not get paid for doing so? Would you stay in a marriage if your spouse stopping having sex, no longer provided you with attention or recognition because "you should?" Most of us would not.

"OK, then, why not limit reinforcers for others to recognition and praise?" The reason is that traditional reinforcers do not work well with some individuals, and not at all with others. We need to focus on what is, rather than how things should be, and recognize that each person has different skills and what works for them as reinforcers is not always the same for others. While many will respond to recognition and praise, not all will. Thus, we need to find what *will* work for them and use them temporarily while helping to develop more natural consequences, such as recognition and praise, into reinforcers for those whom they do not currently function as such.

USING EXTRINSIC REINFORCERS. "Why should we use such intrusive reinforcers. Why not just praise?" Because praise does not work for everyone as a reinforcer or to motivate behavior change. Recognizing individual differences, we cannot expect the same consequences to work for everyone. Many behaviors will bring their own reinforcing consequences. For example, learning to read is not a reinforcing activity for all children. It is not until children are able to experience the natural reinforcers of reading, entertainment, information, and knowledge, that reading provides its own reinforcers.

Because of individual differences in cognitive, physical, and social development, different individuals are at different developmental levels. As a result, sometimes we need to temporarily use extrinsic reinforcers, such as preferred foods, money, or access to activities to motivate others to work toward a goal. However, this type of intervention is temporary, as our goal is always to help people "become less and less dependent on material or other contrived reinforcers. Programs must start where individuals are and gradually help them move up the developmental ladder" (Mayer, 2000, p. 14). As Seeman (1994) has generally pointed out, "children are first motivated by extrinsic rewards (food, toys), then emotional rewards, (approval, grades), and finally, if they attain this, intrinsic rewards (a feeling of pride, self-satisfaction, enjoying it for its own sake)." As a result of such individual differences, we use preference assessments to help us determine what consequences are likely to serve as reinforcers, and use various contrived reinforcers when natural consequences fail to help an individual learn.

When consulting with organizations it is not uncommon to hear from upper management that they question why they need to reinforce employees for engaging in work that "they are already getting paid for." While it is true that the employees are earning a wage, we know as behavior analysts that the delay from when the response occurs and the reinforcer is delivered is problematic and generally the wage does *not* actually reinforce the behavior of working. Moreover, generally the pay is not dependent on the actual work but just showing up to work. Thus, we need to get upper management to see the benefit of providing additional reinforcers for the behavior they want to see, instead of focusing on "shoulds."

USING EXTINCTION. "I don't believe in withholding my love and attention at any time with my child." We have encountered some consultees who object strongly to withholding reinforcement to inappropriate behavior. A case familiar to us, was a mother whose brother had autism. Her parents would often ignore her brother completely for long periods of time following his misbehavior. We found it helpful to point out that what her parents used was an inappropriate variation of timeout and not at all what we were suggesting. Her parents were not giving her brother any opportunities to gain their attention appropriately, and we agreed with her that what her parents used was not appropriate. We stressed that it was important to not ignore her child, but to give him lots of love and attention throughout the day, except immediately following a misbehavior. We also stressed *how* this approach was different from what her parents used with her brother. This helped, but she still had some difficulty not communicating her love and attention during the misbehavior. It took continued discussions and feedback discussing the data on the effects of following misbehavior with such reinforcement, and reinforced practice in using extinction, before she felt comfortable with using extinction. Also, sometimes, people feel like if they "let the person engage in the problem behavior" and don't say anything to them about why it is wrong, they are giving permission for the person to engage in the behavior. It is important to point out that withholding attention contingent on problem behavior is *not* providing permission to engage in such behavior. Consultees may also feel social pressure to provide attention when the client misbehaves out of fear of others' judgement.

USING PUNISHMENT. Some consultees would rather use punishment—in fact some have no problem using punishment—while others, like us, do have issues with its use. It is not uncommon to hear parents say "I should just spank him and then he won't do X anymore" or hear managers say "I should just fire them." A major issue that many consultees are not familiar with is the long-term effects of punishment. These long-term effects started becoming obvious based on research findings a number of years ago. For example, Martin (1974) did a study on the effects of punishment on youngsters' behavior on seeking out knowledge. He found that young children's rate of on-task behavior was greater when they were reprimanded for being off-task than when they were praised for staying on-task. Such immediate gratifying results obviously reinforce the use of punishment (reprimands and other punishing consequences) by consultees, such as parents and teachers. However, his data also showed that these same children later avoided the activities that were associated with the reprimands but did continue to engage in activities for which they had been praised. Also, as you know, not only does punishment result in escape/avoidance reactions (including tardiness, truancies, and dropouts in schools), but it also often results in aggression (e.g., violence, assaults, and vandalism), and lowered self-statements of competences and value of self. Critics also see it as dehumanizing. And, as pointed out by many (e.g., Mayer et al., 2019; Pelios et al., 1999), punitive approaches are no more effective than antecedent and reinforcement-based approaches when based on the behavior's function. The use of punishment, then, should be minimized, as stipulated by the Behavior Analysis Certification Board's Professional and Ethic Compliance Code of Behavior Analysts (March, 2016): "Behavior analysts recommend reinforcement rather than punishment whenever possible" (Code 4.08). Moreover, Kopelman and Schneller demonstrated that a mixed contingency, including reinforcement and punishment, was not only better at controlling abuse of overtime and unscheduled absences, but it resulted in better organizational morale than by just using punishment. We believe punishment should be used only when all parties agree that it is necessary due to the severity of the behavior (e.g., presenting danger to self and/or others) and an appropriate replacement behavior is being taught and reinforced. For various methods of creating a positive classroom environment, in place of a punitive one, see Mayer (2020).

TREATING ONE DIFFERENTLY FROM OTHERS. "How can I give Debbie candy for being on-task but not my other students?" "How can I allow Jose more time to complete his session notes than I do the other RBTs?" This type of question is a common one when there is more than a single person in the same setting. When you set up a special reinforcement program for an individual, how do you handle such questions?

Because each situation is different from another, consider the following strategies:

- Often, the others in the environment are relieved that your client is finally getting some help. Maybe the client will no longer be such a distraction and annoyance. If this is the case, no program modifications are necessary.
- However, if one or more others do complain, stress that the special reinforcers that the client is receiving are for the improvement or progress that is made. And then point out that: "If you have an area we can agree on that you, too, need to improve on, I'll be happy to set up a similar program for you."
- Some have found it helpful to modify the program so that the client can earn the special activity or item(s) not only for him or herself, but for the others as well (e.g., group contingencies).

PROGRAM EFFECTIVENESS. Sometimes you will find that your consultee is not convinced that the intervention program is all that effective. We have found that a good way to help convince them of the program's relative effectiveness is to have them go back to what they were doing during baseline conditions (i.e., use a withdrawal design). Show the consultee the graphed data of the the client's behavior (how the behavior is reverting back to baseline levels. The behavior does not need to go back all the way to the baseline level, just enough to show the effect). This demonstrates to consultees the effects that their previous behavior has on the client. You then ask them to re-implement the intervention program that they questioned. Again, point out using the graphed data how the behavior is again improving as a result of the intervention.

ADDITIONAL STRATEGIES FOR ENHANCING FIDELITY OF IMPLEMENTATION

Select Goals Collaboratively

Goal-setting is a management method designed to encourage personnel to try harder—to *stretch* toward a new level, or to maintain a high level of performance. It is usually best to select goals jointly, as involving those who will be implementing the programs in goal selection "can aid the selection of more rapidly achievable goals; those apt to be achieved more rapidly and supported by the natural environment" (Mayer et al., 2019. p. 73). Goal selection, then, is an important step forward to achieving behavior change. Once goals are selected, first for clients, then for consultees, and agreed to, it is most important to immediately reinforce any action that will result in the eventual attainment of the goal.

Goal selection for your consultees occurs as you discuss and agree upon the interventions to be used with the client. *The implementation of the interventions becomes the goals for the consultee.* One general goal we try to work toward with most consultees involves an increased use of positive reinforcement and a decreased use of punishment. For as Rasmussen and Newland (2008) point out, punishment and reinforcement are not equal in their impact on behavior. Research now indicates that it takes about three to four reinforcing consequences to counter the effects of a punishing consequence. For youngsters with emotional and behavioral disorders (EBD), a nine-to-one ratio appears to be necessary to counteract the effects of the punishment and to improve their behavior (Caldarella, Larsen, Williams, Wills, & Wehby, 2019). Similarly, Robinson and Peter (2019) found that 10-year-olds with ADHD and who engaged in chronic, severe problem behavior reduced such behavior *and spent more time on academic responding* once they began accumulating reinforcers throughout the session. Thus, it may be that those with more severe disorders, or those who are at risk, need more reinforcement to counter the effects of punishment and/or the lack of reinforcement. It appears that *the more punishers (timeout, criticizing, disapproval, fines, swats, restrictions, etc.) and periods of non-reinforcement youngsters have experienced, the more reinforcers they need to help prevent inappropriate behaviors and to promote more time in academic activities.*

Often, improvement is gradual. See Box 4.1 (Mayer et al., 2019) on the next page for a hypothetical example that illustrates the process of gradually increasing the criterion level for achieving the goal.

Use Instructions and Explanations

By this point, you have 1) developed a level of rapport; 2) identified your goal(s) and intervention(s); and 3) discussed and resolved any concerns your consultee might have expressed. We now move on to helping consultees begin to implement your jointly selected interventions.

Instructions and explanations are commonly used to help people learn how to start doing various activities. When providing instructions and explanations to your consultee, be sure not to present too much. You do not want to overwhelm your consultee. Also, as pointed out below, when instructions are used, they should be followed by modeling, unless it is behavior you know that your consultee can readily do because you have seen it occur before.

USE COMPREHENSIBLE LANGUAGE. Review the discussion in Chapter 1 on this important factor that can influence the consultee's program implementation.

Use Modeling and Provide Practice

After you have explained what will need to be done and why, it is best to show, or model, how the intervention should be implemented. Modeling has been shown to be more effective than direct instructions or group discussions in produc-

Box 4.1: An Example of Goal-Setting

Especially when employee injuries are minor, the incidence reports required by law and by Port Pembroke's Paper Products' insurance carriers are often submitted much later than required by company and governmental policy. To address this deficiency, the Director of Operations assembles the supervisors and elaborates upon all the reasons why rapid reporting is important (legal, ethical, monetary, and so on). She then displays a graph of the percentage of reports turned in on time (see figure below). The gap between the present level and perfection is far too wide to reasonably expect perfection to be achieved overnight. So the group decides to set a goal of 55 percent for the next week. This is indicated with an arrow on the graph. During the following two weeks, the group meets the goal and the manager congratulates everyone. Next they discuss whether to raise the goal still higher, to 75 percent. All agree. She draws a line at the 75 percent level. They reach it twice. Heartened by their success, they decide to go for 100 percent. But the team only reaches that goal once during the next four weeks. After discussing the matter and realizing that emergencies such as absent supervisors and various unanticipated crises might occur, they consent to lowering the final level to 90 percent. By the end of the nineteenth week, they have succeeded twice. "That's probably as high as any program like ours should be expected to sustain," the manager announces. "As you can see, the effort you've all made has really paid off. So, in appreciation, during the lunch break this Friday, there'll be a pizza party—on us!"

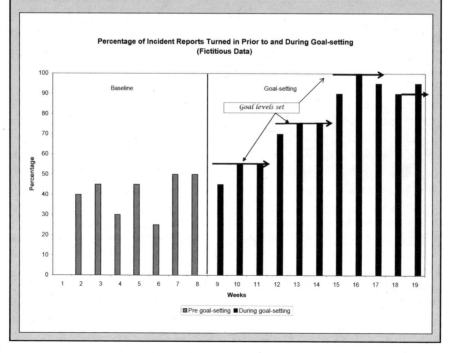

ing consultee change as far back as 1969 (Johnson & Brown). It is a powerful method for not only increasing the occurrence of behaviors but also for teaching new behaviors.

A modeling technique that we have taught consultants to use effectively is to present the following rule or guideline to their consultees: "When you see a non-serious infraction occur, rather than attempting to punish the infraction, model what he or she could do and/or say in place of the infraction. Then, ask the person to imitate the modeled behavior. Once the person imitates the modeled behavior, be sure to reinforce that act of imitation." If in a classroom or another group setting, immediately following the infraction, look for other youngsters who are engaged in the appropriate behavior and reinforce those acsts. For example, if Maria is off-task, reinforce (e.g., compliment) students who are in their seats working. Be sure to vary the models that you select. Then, of course, as soon as Maria is in her seat working, complement her behavior too. This same procedure can be utilized in a factory or work setting as well. Basically, pick several model employees and be sure to reinforce employees for imitating the reinforced behavior of the model employees. Moreover, make sure you are modeling the behavior that you want the consultee to engage in. For example, it is common when doing an observation with the consultee to make sure to model how to reinforce appropriate behavior of others (students, employees, etc.) by showing the consultee how to deliver contingent praise.

Video modeling also has been shown to be very helpful in helping consultees learn various interventions. For example, investigators (Taber, Lambright, & Luiselli, 2017) displayed a video model of staff interacting with a youngster. The video showed a novel care provider offering labeled praise in a form that encouraged a reciprocal response (e.g., "You are doing a good job staying in your seat, aren't you?"). After viewing the video just once, the consultees increased their use of labeled praise that encouraged reciprocal responses. Video modeling also has been used to provide individualized feedback to parents (Phaneuf & McIntyre, 2007). The mother and consultant viewed video tapes of the mother interacting with her child during playtime. The consultant stopped the video and praised the mother's behavior every two minutes, provided the mother had not done anything inappropriate during the previous interval. If an inappropriate behavior occurred, the video was stopped and the mother was asked to identify preferable alternatives. The consultant praised and modeled those suggestions and then asked the parent to role-play the skills. Praise or corrective feedback followed as merited. As a result, the parents improved their parenting skills.

When using instructions and modeling, be very careful that what you are presenting is neither too complex to be understood or imitated. *A behavior is more likely to be rapidly understood and imitated if it contains some components the individual has previously learned, and if the new components are neither too many nor presented too rapidly.* Some research has demonstrated the use of video prompting the links of behavior chains versus a single video model of the entire chain with success. Thus, if the behavior consists of multiple steps and is complex, it might be a good idea to use video prompting rather than video modeling (Cannella-Malone et al., 2003). With this procedure, you would create a video of each step and use behavior chaining to train the entire skill.

Use Behavioral Skills Training (BST)

BST consists of *a combination of instructions, modeling, rehearsal, and feedback.* Modeling is most effective when used as part of BST. BST is a very useful training method for teaching interventions to program implementers—your consultees. So, once you have instructed and reinforced a model's behavior, follow the reinforcement with role playing and/or practice and feedback. Providing an opportunity to practice new skills followed by reinforcing feedback improves the likelihood of your consultees actually using the intervention correctly.

Provide a Checklist

Checklists can serve several purposes. They can function as a prompt to remind consultees what they need to do, and they have been shown to help improve treatment integrity or fidelity; in other words, *they promote implementing the intervention accurately*. They appear most useful when the intervention has multiple components or when there are several tasks that need to be completed. For example, Goings et al. (2019) used a checklist with feedback to assist teachers to improve their classroom appearance and organization which included items such as putting away toys and electronic devices and placing chairs under tables. As a result, the classrooms improved their appearance and organization. Basically, checklists are like a task analysis of what is to be done. For example, you and a teacher might agree that students who do the following will be complemented: enter the classroom orderly, start their work quickly, work quietly on task during the period, and wrap-up in an orderly fashion. A task list would consist of:

> **Check off each of the following as completed**
> 1. _____ Reinforced entering orderly (walking and not talking loudly)
> 2. _____ Reinforced starting their work within 10 seconds of sitting down
> 3. _____ Reinforced quietly working on their assignment
> 4. _____ Reinforced putting away their materials quickly and quietly

Checklists are also great for managers to use when they are managing employees. For example, a shift manager at a factory might use the following checklist:

1. _____ Reinforced employee for being engaged in work task
2. _____ Reinforced employee for clean work station
3. _____ Reinforced employee for wearing safety attire
4. _____ Reinforced employee for following safety guidelines

Check lists are not only important for teaching consultees' what to do, but they also are great for monitoring, or helping to determine if the consultees are doing what they have been taught to do (Bacon, Fulton, & Malott, 1982; Burg Reid, & Lattmore, 1979; Mouzakitis, Codding, & Tryon, 2015). They also can increase implementers' awareness when they do something incorrectly, therefore minimizing the amount of corrective feedback that is needed.

Promote Self-Monitoring

Suggesting that your consultee self-monitor is similar to using a checklist. Self-monitoring, though, can be used on a single behavior or on multiple behaviors. If a teacher was to self-monitor the behaviors listed in the checklist above, a column could be made for each the four behaviors, and the teacher would place a check-mark in the correct column each time she did the behavior. For example, if she reinforced at least three students who entered orderly, three checks would be in that column.

Self-monitoring by itself sometimes can help promote desired behavior change. For example, Cook et al. (2016) asked teachers to self-monitor their ratios of positive-to-negative interactions with their students. This strategy resulted not only in more positive and fewer negative interactions, but it also resulted in fewer classroom disruptions and increased academic engagement by the students.

Be Present and Supportive

The first few days of implementing an intervention are the most crucial. What occurs and how you handle it can determine the success or failure of the program. Therefore, it is best if you arrange to be present when the intervention is first implemented, and frequently during the first week or two. As we emphasize in Chapter 6, do not harp on examples of poor performance, but provide heavy doses of positive recognition for program implementation process and effort. Otherwise you run the risk that your presence will become aversive, resulting in you becoming someone to be avoided by the consultee.

Your presence can serve as a prompt to implement the program. Misunderstandings and inconsistencies can be identified and corrected. In addition, by being present you can help solve problems that may develop. For example, you and the consultee agree to implement a modeling program. You observe that the model's behavior is reinforced but the act of imitating the model's behavior is not. Observing this omission, you can cue the consultee to reinforce the behavior, and/or model it yourself to prompt the behavior to occur in future applications of modeling. Here is another example: a consultant and teacher set up a response cost penalty of four points for any act of swearing. All involved youngsters were notified of this penalty for swearing. While the consultant was observing, a youngster let out a string of swear words and was fined four points. As a result, the youngster became very disruptive. The consultant then suggested that the response cost program be changed. When any youngster was fined and then immediately got back to work without complaints after being fined, one-half the fine would be returned. This program modification seemed to solve such problems in her classroom. Thus, *be available to catch inconsistencies, misunderstandings and resolve problems that may develop.*

Sometimes it may be impossible for you to be present when it would be helpful. If you supervise Registered Behavior Technicians (RBTs), they can be taught to provide the appropriate reinforcement and consultation. Or, if no RBT is available, like for a classroom, perhaps you could obtain the services of a counselor, school psychologist, or administrator to help provide such in-classroom services.

Provide Other Cues

It is often hard to break old habits and start new ones. Most consultees have a variety of responsibilities and demands on their time and attention. Sometimes cues can help them to recall what and when they need to engage in a different pattern of behavior. We have found that it is often helpful to discuss with your consultee the fact that it is often hard to recall to implement a program that one is not used to doing. Jointly working out a cueing system is often helpful. You both might decide that you will hold up a colored piece of paper, or give some physical sign such as a head nod, to remind your consultee that now is the time to reinforce, or to ignore, the current behavior. You might create a signal, such as tugging your ear when a supervisor is to provide a supervisee praise or feedback. Also, it has been shown that if you and your consultee decide to use a point or token system, giving points or tokens can also serve as a prompt or discriminative stimulus to socially reinforce an individual's behavior.

If you find your consultee feeling awkward using praise as a reinforcer, you might try helping your consultee coming up with specific times and situations to use praise. For example, when working with a high school teacher who was resisting socially reinforcing his students' appropriate behavior due to it feeling awkward, instead of natural, the consultant and teacher identified specific instances when he would use praise: 1) During the first minute of the period he would reinforce at least one randomly selected student for demonstrating a desirable behavior as entering the room appropriately (e.g., walking in quietly and immediately taking seat). 2) Twice during the class, he would walk around for five minutes and provide praise for being on-task, asking appropriate questions, and helping one another. As he increased his reinforcement, the consultant was able to show, using data, how much his class was improving. Eventually, he began to feel comfortable using social reinforcers, and started on his own to use them at other times of the day and with his other class periods. He also reported enjoying teaching more. Mutually-derived structure (with reinforcing feedback from the consultant) appears to increase the use of social reinforcement by infrequent users.

Sometimes, role playing will help the consultee to get comfortable delivering praise. And/or you might give the consultee a list of things to say (e.g., "X, it is great that you are wearing your safety glasses, it really helps"; "X, great job shutting down the line when you need to step away"; "X, it is so important to not be distracted when the assembly line is running, and I noticed you are doing a great job") and practice the statements until the consultee is comfortable with them.

It is helpful, then, initially to provide abundant cues and give feedback until the consultee's behavior is established. Don't just rely reminders to insure strategy implementation.

Ensure Contextual Fit

As mentioned before, **treatment integrity** (also known as **fidelity of implementation** or **procedural fidelity**) involves ensuring that *everyone involved carries out and supports the intervention as planned*. We have mentioned strategies throughout this chapter that you can use to help promote treatment integrity, including joint goal and intervention selection which was introduced in Chapter 2. Here we will address contextual fit, an important consideration that also can help you promote treatment integrity. Without treatment integrity, your interventions are not likely to be effective in producing the client behavior change you and your consultee seek.

Interventions that you jointly select with your consultee need to have **contextual fit**. This means that *they need to fit the skills, resources, schedules, and values of your consultee* (Horner, 1994). Many behavior analysts and other consultants are taught to select the intervention that has the most data supporting its effectiveness (e.g., evidence-based research). However, if that intervention does not fit your consultee's skills, resources, schedules, and/or values, it is not likely to be implemented as planned. As *shaping* illustrates, you have to start at the functional level of your consultee. *This can mean that your consultee is not able at this time to implement the most effective intervention.* You may have to gradually help them to understand, accept, and gradually increase their skills before they are able to implement a highly effective program. The high school teacher above was worked with to increase his use of social praise gradually. Here are two examples that use **shaping** (i.e., *differentially reinforcing succes-*

sive approximations toward the behavioral objective) to help the consultee move toward implementing the most effective intervention:

> Mrs. Jones, an 8th grade teacher, asked for help with her classroom in which various misbehaviors were common. The consultant's observations indicated that Mrs. Jones was quite skillful in identifying and administering punishment to individual students when they misbehaved, but that she did not use reinforcement when they were working — a baseline of zero. In discussing the possible strategies, the teacher indicated that it would be impossible for her to reinforce individual students for their positive behavior because she had 33 students and most of them were disruptive in the class. (However, she was very skillful at punishing individual students frequently throughout the class period.) After the overwhelming nature of the situation was reflected, the consultant sought to jointly seek out a jointly acceptable starting goal. Because the teacher was skillful in identifying misbehaviors and using punishers (e.g., "Johnnie sit down!"; "Mary be quiet!"; "Give me that!") the first step the consultant followed was to build on the teacher's current skills. They first discussed and then he demonstrated how she could use a modified response cost program. Each student started off the day with a total of ten points listed on a point card on their desks. Each time Mrs. Jones observed a misbehavior she crossed out one of the points. Near the end of the period, students could exchange the points for time in a reinforcing activity center, which the consultant helped the teacher set up in the rear of her classroom. The consultant frequently stopped by Mrs. Jones' classroom to assist her, to answer any questions she might have, and to reinforce her efforts in implementing the program. What were the student' reactions? They reported they liked the program because "Mrs. Jones doesn't yell at us much anymore."
>
> Once the first phase of the shaping program began to work, the consultant introduced the next sub-goal toward developing a reinforcing classroom environment. He suggested that when the class goes for 10 to 15 minutes without misbehaviors (which they were starting to do) the teacher could reinforce the whole class's behavior with social reinforcement and an extra point by saying, "I sure am pleased with the way all of you are working. You deserve an extra point on your cards. Go ahead and put a plus one on your card." The teacher agreed and implemented the plan. Again, the consultant carefully monitored the progress and socially reinforced the teacher whenever he could, as he would continue to do at each successive step toward the goal of increasing the use of positive reinforcement. Once the second goal was successful (i.e., student behavior results were positive, and so were reactions to the teacher's use of positive reinforcement), a third goal was implemented. The teacher was asked if she could socially

reinforce one student, Jose, when she saw him at work, and communicated to her that Jose appears to seek out her attention. The teacher again agreed to implementing this next step.

Once the behavior of reinforcing Jose was established, another student was added, who, it was pointed out, was very similar to Jose. (Similarity was stressed to enhance the likelihood that the teacher would generalize (see Chapter 7) her use of reinforcement. Soon, other students were added in a similar fashion, then small groups of students, until the program was changed from students being given ten points and penalized during the period to both groups and individual students earning their points for constructive classroom behavior. An aversive classroom situation was changed eventually to a positive one in a few short months, and students volunteered a number of positive comments about their teacher and the changes that had taken place.

Here is another example showing how you might start based on the consultee's skills. Note how the goals keep shifting, starting at a point that the consultee can do, and gradually increasing, with the help of the consultant, until a more desired intervention has been achieved:

A fourth-grade teacher was having difficulty getting a student to attend to directions, explanations, and assignments, and to reduce his disruptive classroom behavior (e.g., yelling out, throwing things). The teacher seldom used positive reinforcement. However, both agreed that a heavy reinforcement program was needed, and that the intervention would be too difficult for the teacher to implement all the time. The first goal that was set involved increasing the teacher's proximity to her pupils. Through observation it was discovered that proximity had an inhibitory effect on the student's disruptive behavior. Thus, teacher was to locate herself near him whenever possible. This first step resulted in a slight unexpected increase in the praise she gave the student for appropriate behaviors. The next step continued the physical proximity, but added an effort to increase her delivery of physical positive reinforcement to the child (e.g. smiling, head nodding, physical contact) when he engaged in attending behaviors. Her use of proximity and physical reinforcement increased once the consultant started providing regular feedback and praise for her implementing these goals. After the second goal was accomplished, the teacher was asked to praise the student's desired behaviors (a list of socially reinforcing comments were provided the teacher and the consultant role-played their use during several role-playing sessions). The comments were to be paired with the proximity and the physical reinforcement program already in progress. Her use of reinforcement further increased. The student's attending behavior increased from 30 percent to 75 percent. His disruptive behaviors decreased from 45 percent to 7 percent. To maintain this program, the consultant was careful to keep regular contact with the teacher.

The above examples illustrate several important points. Different initial goals, steps, or approximations were selected in each example even though the terminal goals were similar This occurred because the teachers were at different skill levels in using reinforcers and aversives. When starting a program, the point in the consultee's repertoire closest to the goal behavior should be selected as the first step or criterion for reinforcement. In other words, *the intervention strategy selected for the client must not be too different initially from what the consultee is doing or has done in the past.* A strategy is not likely to be successful unless the selected steps or approximations are tailored to the individual's behavioral repertoire. For example, another consultee might not have needed reinforcement divided into physical and praise areas as the teacher did in our second example. However, this teacher did appear to need this extra step to achieve success. If the initial step or approximation selected is too different or too large, the program may not be successful. If difficulty occurs, back up! Try selecting a smaller step and start again. In other words, use your knowledge of shaping.

Here is a non-educational example of using shaping. A behavioral agency was having a hard time getting their RBTs (Registered Behavioral Technicians) to take data every session, enter the data after the session, and update graphs weekly. The BCBA who was supervising the RBTs said he didn't know what to do any more—he had been giving the RBTs feedback and threatening to fire them, but nothing was working. The agency had an outside consultant that met with the BCBAs on a monthly basis to provide consultation. At the meeting with the consultant, the BCBA (consultee) and consultant developed a plan for checking the RBTs entering the data, monitoring their graphs, and providing feedback. At first the consultee felt that he did not have the time to implement such a plan, and besides, the RBTs should just do their job (notice the resistance). The consultant first addressed the resistance and then decided that it would be a good idea to shape the consultee's behavior. The consultant went over how to provide feedback, modeled it with him, and gave the consultee feedback on how he did. It was agreed that the BCBA consultee would check to see if data were recorded and entered for all their RBTs at the end of each day and not check on the graphs for two weeks. In addition, the BCBA was to record the amount of time it took him to check up on each RBT he supervised (N=15). The BCBA was successful at leaving 30 minutes at the end of the day to check to see if the RBTs had indeed collected and entered their data. He said on average it took him about 20 minutes to do so and another 10 minutes to send out emails to the RBTs that had not taken and/or entered their data. The consultant met with the BCBA consultee and made sure to not only reinforce the checking up on the RBT's data entry, but for also providing feedback to the RBTs. In addition, the consultant reminded the BCBA consultee the importance of following the feedback steps to ensure reinforcement for the RBTs. The next step was then implemented, wherein, the BCBA consultee was not only checking on the data entry daily, but was now going to reserve another 20 minutes at the end of the week to check that graphs were updated by the RBT. The consultee and consultant also developed a data check sheet and feedback form to give to the RBTs on a weekly basis that summarized the percentage of days they had taken and entered their data and noted if the graph was updated. After another two weeks, the consultant checked in with the consultee to see how things were going. The consultee told the consultant that not only were his RBTs taking data and entering the data but they were updating the graphs as well. He also felt like the RBTs were finally responding to his feedback in a positive fashion and that he didn't need to threaten them with the loss of their job to get them to do things. At this point although the BCBA consultee was excited, he did have a concern that if he got more RBTs, he wasn't sure he would be able to check up on each RBT every day regarding data entry and every week for updating the graph. At this point, the consultant and consultee developed a check-up schedule for each of his RBTs so that each RBT data entry and graphs were checked randomly at least two times a month. Once the consultee was doing these random checks on entering session data and graph updates, the RBTs were doing their jobs, the consultee was not spending a lot of time and all were happy with the results.

As Horner (1994) pointed out some time ago, "*The goal is not to find the one true intervention, but to find an intervention that is effective and will be implemented by the people in the setting*" (p. 403). A safe way to begin is by selecting evidence-based strategies as similar as possible to ongoing practices, especially those that build on the strengths and skills the consultees already possess. When given a choice, then, *assign high priority to interventions that not only have supporting evidence, but that your consultees can implement with relative ease, are acceptable to them, and address their concerns, while promoting improved client adjustment, adaptation, competence, or habilitation.*

Also, as Mayer et al. (2019) have explained, *what consultees say and what they actually can and cannot do may be different*. "The best tactic is to sample the individual's actual level of performance over time, then, and build upon that baseline" (p. 45). In other words, it is often best initially to *jointly select interventions that are not too different from what the consultee is doing or has done in the past.*

To further enhance the effectiveness of moving from one goal to another, use various prompts, such as directions, models, cues, role-playing, or any antecedent that will help foster the occurrence of the next desired step or approximation. In each of the examples described previously, the consultant used a variety of such antecedents. Do not wait for the next step or approximation to occur. Prompt the occurrence of the next step.

If you have difficulty determining contextual fit, or just want more related information on the family you are working with, consider Albin's et al. (1996) *goodness-of-fit* assessment questionnaire[1]. Its 12 items are designed to help you determine if your selected intervention complements the family goals and expectations, lifestyle, implementation effort/time, and sustainability.

Observe the Effects of Potential Reinforcers

We mention many possible reinforcing sources and various reinforcers for the consultee's behavior (e.g., see Chapter 6). However, like with clients, do not just arbitrarily use any of them. A potential reinforcer used arbitrarily or inappropriately can backfire and serve as a punisher. For example, bringing visitors and/or supervisors to observe the consultee's skills. Some consultees find such an activity aversive or punishing. Bringing visitors and or supervisors into one of those situations could result in the consultee refusing to work with you anymore. Be sensitive to the effects that any potential reinforcer may have on your consultee's behavior. Be sure to discuss their application before using them. In other words, the reinforcers you finally select should be mutually agreed upon. Also, observe their effects to determine if they are truly reinforcing. When applied, if the consultee smiles, and/or maintains or increases the frequency of implementing the program, you have some evidence that what was jointly selected is truly reinforcing. However, if the consultee starts to avoid you, withdraws, responds aggressively, or decreases use of the intervention, you have evidence that it was not reinforcing but was probably punishing. Terminate its use immediately. Confer again with the consultee, apologize, admit your mistake, and re-negotiate what are used as reinforcers.

SUMMARY AND CONCLUSIONS

Given the likelihood of contacting resistance when consulting, it is important to identify resistance when it occurs, assess the contingencies supporting it, and use behavioral strategies to overcome it. It is also important to determine how one would react to some common forms of resistance that you may encounter including experiencing difficulty with implementation, finding time, the analogy of thinking reinforcement is bribery, issues with using extinction and punishment, and treating people differently. Using goal setting, BST, checklists, and self-monitoring are ways to increase the consultee's treatment integrity. Moreover, it is important to be present and supportive while providing cues, contextual fit, and shaping to help promote a consultee's treatment-fidelity.

---

[1] You can see the survey on the Web : Albin's Goodness of Fit Survey

ACTIVITIES

1. Working with your consultee, describe how you jointly selected goals.
2. As you jointly selected interventions, describe how you: (a) addressed any concerns that were raised; (b) ensured contextual fit; (c) selected reinforcers for the consultee (and specify what they are and what evidence you have of their effectiveness); and once the interventions were selected, (d) how you used BST.
3. Develop a checklist and show it to a peer for feedback.
4. Describe how you were available for program implementation.
5. Come up with some praise statements you can have your consultee practice.

Chapter 5

Determining Fidelity of Implementation

Promoting implementation fidelity was discussed in Chapter 4. Here the focus is on determining the actual level of implementation fidelity. If we want to say that a specific intervention is responsible for behavior change, we must demonstrate a functional relationship between the behavior and the intervention. Part of demonstrating that functional relationships is demonstrating that the intervention was implemented as planned (i.e., with treatment fidelity). We also know that if procedures are not implemented as intended, the risk of intervention failure can occur. Generally speaking, the higher the treatment integrity, the more effective an intervention is (e.g., Carroll, Kodak, & Fisher, 2013; Cook et al., 2010; DiGennero et al., 2007; Fryling, Wallace, & Yassine, 2012; Noell, Gresham, & Gansle, 2002). As a behavioral consultant, one of your main responsibilities will be ensuring that interventions are being implemented as planned. Just like other avenues in behavior analysis, it is not sufficient to assume or take someone's word for it that an intervention is being implemented as planned—you must operationally define what is meant by implementing the intervention as planned, set up a measurement system to assess and capture if the behavior of implementing the intervention as planned is occurring or not, and provide remedial procedures to ensure adherence if not observed.

OPERATIONALLY DEFINING CORRECT AND INCORRECT IMPLEMENTATION

Before treatment integrity, or fidelity of implementation, measures can be taken, it is important to operationally define what behavior will be considered correct implementation and what behavior will be considered incorrect implementation. Both errors of omission (not performing a step) and commission (adding a step) must be considered when defining correct and incorrect implementation of an intervention. By operationally defining errors of omission, common errors can proactively be addressed (once errors occur, they are much more likely to recur). Thus, initially minimizing potential errors may help your consultee avoid engaging in an incorrect behavior chain during intervention. For example, a teacher is implementing a differential reinforcement of alternative behavior (DRA) intervention in which the teacher will only allow breaks from work when students raise their hand and ask for a break. Part of the intervention plan includes not allowing a break if a student does not ask for a break or engages in a problem behavior. Would you score the teacher providing praise to students for working hard on their problems as incorrect or correct implementation of the procedure? If you said incorrect, you are correct, it would be an error of commission according to the description of the procedure above. This example points out the need for a task analysis of the entire program. One way to define correct and incorrect behaviors is to task analyze the plan (i.e., have a detailed step-by-step description of the plan) that has all possible behaviors of the student and what to do and all the behaviors of the teacher (see Chapter 4 on Creating a Checklist). One advantage of task analyzing the procedure is that the task analysis could also serve as your recording method for measuring correct and incorrect implementation. Let's look at a task analysis of a common procedure used to treat non-compliance and problem behavior maintained by escape from demands (3-Step Compliance; see Figure 5.1).

You will notice that correct behavior for the consultee includes both errors of omission and commission. For example, if after the consultee hand-over-hand guides the student to comply and then delivers praise, that is an incorrect response, thus taking errors of commission into account. It also paints a picture of the various topographies of the maladaptive behavior the intervention may trigger and provides examples of how to react to each potential behavior.

Sometimes the jointly decided goal might be to focus only on increasing the use of positive reinforcement. If that is the case, a simple checklist, similar to the one illustrated in Chapter 4, can be used. Just check off each time praise was delivered for each activity (in this case, not praising the identified target behaviors would be considered incorrect behavior). This is what Mayer et al. (1983; 1993) did when attempting to increase the frequency of reinforcer delivery in various classrooms to help make the classroom environments more positive.

Once the procedure is task analyzed with respect to correct and incorrect behavior of the consultee given the individual's possible behavior, it is time to measure, calculate, and summarize treatment integrity.

Step	Consultee Behavior	Child Behavior	Consultee Behavior	Correct/Incorrect
1.	Demand Presentation	Present S^d		C I N/A
1a		Complies	Praise	C I N/A
1b		No Response	Waits 5 s and goes to Step 2 and does NOT praise	C I N/A
1c		Engages in problem behavior	Hand over hand guides completion of task and does NOT praise	C I N/A
2.	Model Presentation	Consultee presents S^d while modeling compliance		C I N/A
		Complies	Praise	C I N/A
		No response	Waits 5 s and goes to Step 3 and does NOT praise	C I N/A
		Engages in problem behavior	Hand over hand guides completion of task and does NOT praise	C I N/A
				C I N/A
3.	Guides Compliance	Hand over hand guides completion of task		C I N/A
		Complies with guidance	Completes guided compliance and does NOT deliver praise	C I N/A
		Struggles with hand over hand	Completes guided compliance and does NOT deliver praise	C I N/A

Figure 5.1 Task Analysis of 3-Step Compliance Procedure

MEASURING AND REPORTING TREATMENT INTEGRITY

Using a task analyzed intervention table as described in the previous section is important for taking reliable and valid data on the fidelity of implementation. As a consultant, it will be imperative to use the task analyzed procedure to record the behavior of the consultee. While watching the consultee implementing the procedure, record correct, incorrect, or not applicable with respect to what the consultee does in relation to the individual. After taking data on correct (C), incorrect (I), or not applicable (N/A), to summarize you would add up the number of correct behaviors and divide by number of correct and incorrect behaviors, and multiply by 100. This gives you the percentage of treatment integrity score. Use the above task analysis to record treatment integrity on the following scenarios and then calculate Mrs. Busser's treatment integrity score.

Mrs. Busser tells Matt it is time to pick up the toys in the kitchen station ("Matt, it is time to pick up. Please put the can of beans on the shelf."). Matt and Mary continue to pretend that they are eating food. Mrs. Busser tells Matt again what to do and shows Matt what she wants him to do. Matt, still not wanting to stop playing, ignores Mrs. Busser. Mrs. Busser gently guides Matt to pick up the can and put it on the shelf and tells him "good job cleaning up, Matt."

Compare your scorecard to our scorecard (see Figure 5.2) and see if we agreed on how to score Mrs. Busser's behavior (i.e., our interobserver agreement). Did you get that Mrs. Busser engages in 5 correct response and 1 incorrect response (i.e., providing praise after the student completes guided compliance)? Now let's transform the data we collected into a treatment integrity score: 5 correct responses/5 correct + 1 incorrect = 0.83 X 100 = 83%. Thus Mrs. Busser implemented the 3-Step Protocol with 83 percent treatment integrity.

So how often should treatment integrity be assessed and what treatment integrity score is sufficient? Although there is no stated "rule" for how often one should assess treatment integrity, based upon the recommendations for observing and calculating reliability of measurement, we propose that at least 33 percent of all session or program implementations be checked for treatment integrity. Given the current supervision practices in the field, it would be important to ensure treatment fidelity during all supervised sessions. Again, this 33 percent is probably more important to obtain in the beginning of a program before the program goes into a maintenance mode where a lower percentage would be sufficient.

What is an appropriate or acceptable level of treatment integrity? We can rely on the literature for some answers. We do know that implementing a treatment as planned (i.e., with 100% integrity) is better than not implementing it as planned (i.e., less than 100% integrity). The question is "at what level of treatment integrity errors is harmful or no longer effective?" This question may prove to be idiosyncratic based upon the specific procedure and the specific error.

Step	Consultee Behavior	Child Behavior	Consultee Behavior	Correct/Incorrect
1.	Demand presentation	Present S^d		(C) I N/A
1a		Complies	Praise	C I N/A
1b		No response	Waits 5 s and goes to Step 2 and does NOT praise	(C) I N/A
1c		Engages in problem behavior	Hand over hand guides completion of task and does NOT praise	C I N/A
2.	Model presentation	Consultee presents S^d while modeling compliance		(C) I N/A
2a		Complies	Praise	C I N/A
2b		No response	Waits 5 s and goes to Step 3 and does NOT praise	(C) I N/A
2c		Engages in problem behavior	Hand over hand guides completion of task and does NOT praise	C I N/A
3.	Guides compliance	Hand over hand guides completion of task		(C) I N/A
3a		Complies with guidance	Completes guided compliance and does NOT deliver praise	C I N/A
3b		Struggles with hand over hand	Completes guided compliance and does NOT deliver praise	C I N/A

Figure 5.2 Scored Task Analysis of Mrs. Busser Implementing 3-Step Compliance Procedure

For example, some research on treatment integrity with respect to implementation of differential reinforcement have shown mixed results (Mazaleski, Iwata, Vollmer, Zarcone, & Smith, 1993; Mueller et al., 2003; Worsdell, Iwata, Hanley, Thompson, & Kahng, 2000). Some studies have looked at errors of omission and demonstrated that treatments have retained their efficacy (e.g., Northup, Fisher, Kahng, Harrell, & Kurtz, 1997), while others have looked at errors of commission and demonstrated that decreases in integrity can have detrimental effects on treatment outcomes (e.g., Worsdell, et al. 2000). More recent studies have looked at errors of omission alone, errors of commission alone, and combined errors (e.g., St. Peter Pipkin, Vollmer, & Sloman, 2010). In the St Peter Pipkin, et al. study, they demonstrated that errors involving reinforcing problem behavior during differential reinforcement for alternative behavior were more detrimental than errors related to reinforcing appropriate behavior alone.

Other investigators (Digennaro-Reed, Reed, Baez, & Maguire, 2011) looked at the effects of errors of commission during error-correction procedures during a discrete-trial program. They looked at varying levels of errors (e.g., 0%, 50%, or 100%). Their findings demonstrated equal levels of detrimental effects on learning of students with both the 50 percent and 100 percent errors of commission.

The literature on reduced levels of treatment integrity shows, then, that slight decreases in integrity, both errors of omission and commission, and procedure-specific errors can produce detrimental effects on treatment outcome. Thus, rather than identifying what is a suitable level of treatment integrity, it might be more prudent to focus on what to do if treatment integrity falls short of 100 percent. (Remember, the higher the treatment integrity the more effective the intervention.)

Step	Consultee Behavior	Child Behavior	Consultee Behavior	Correct/Incorrect
1.	Session Prep	Gathers items: items for assessment (5), data sheet (MSWO), timer		C I N/A
2.	MSWO Trial 1	Consultee presents all 5 items in a row and presents S^d "Pick one"		C I N/A
2.a.1.		Picks an item	Delivers item for 30 seconds	C I N/A
2.a.2.		Attempts to pick more than one item	Blocks and represents S^d "pick one"	C I N/A
2.a.3.		Does not respond	Represents S^d "pick one"	C I N/A
2.b.		Picks an item after 2.a.2. or 2.a.3.	Delivers item for 30 seconds	C I N/A
3.	Close Trial 1	Removes item from client and record selection		C I N/A
4.	MSWO Trial 2	Consultee presents all 4 items in a row and presents S^d "Pick one"		C I N/A
4.a.1.		Picks an item	Delivers item for 30 seconds	C I N/A
4.a.2.		Attempts to pick more than one item	Blocks and represents S^d "pick one"	C I N/A
4.a.3.		Does not respond	Represents S^d "pick one"	C I N/A
4.b.		Picks an item after 4.a.2. or 4.a.3.	Delivers item for 30 seconds	C I N/A
5.	Close Trial 2	Removes item from client and record selection		C I N/A

DETERMINING FIDELITY OF IMPLEMENTATION • 73

6.	MSWO Trial 3	Consultee presents all 3 items in a row and presents S^d "Pick one"		C	I	N/A
7.a.1.		Picks an item	Delivers item for 30 seconds	C	I	N/A
7.a.2.		Attempts to pick more than one item	Blocks and represents S^d "pick one"	C	I	N/A
7.a.3.		Does not respond	Represents S^d "pick one"	C	I	N/A
7.b.		Picks an item after 7.a.2.or 7.a.3.	Delivers item for 30 seconds	C	I	N/A
8. Close Trial 3	Removes item from client and record selection			C	I	N/A
9. MSWO Trial 4	Consultee presents all 2 items in a row and presents S^d "Pick one"			C	I	N/A
10.a.1.		Picks an item	Delivers item for 30 seconds	C	I	N/A
10.a.2.		Attempts to pick more than one item	Blocks and represents S^d "pick one"	C	I	N/A
10.a.3.		Does not respond	Represents S^d "pick one"	C	I	N/A
10.b.		Picks an item after 10.a.2.or 10.a.3.	Delivers item for 30 seconds	C	I	N/A
11. Close trial 4	Removes item from client and record selection			C	I	N/A
12. MSWO Trial 5	Consultee presents last items and presents S^d "Pick one"			C	I	N/A
13.a.1.		Picks item	Delivers item for 30 seconds	C	I	N/A
13.a.2.		Does not respond	Represents S^d "pick one"	C	I	N/A

13.b.		Picks item after 13.a.2.	Delivers item for 30 seconds	C	I	N/A
14. Close Trial 4	Removes item from client and record selection			C	I	N/A
15. Calculates percentage for each item (1 divided by trail chosen X100)				C	I	N/A

Here is an example of an integrity check sheet that can be used for checking the integrity of a RBT conducting a preference assessment using a multiple stimulus without replacement (MSWO) format.

WHAT TO DO ABOUT INTEGRITY FAILURES

If upon assessing for treatment integrity, errors of implementation are noted, what can be done? Similar to *Promoting Implementation with Fidelity* (Chapter 4), the best ways to address failures is to take a preventative and proactive approach. Preventative measures such as addressing concerns about aspects of the intervention that are not being implemented correctly, re-training on aspects of the procedure using BST or competency-based training (i.e., re-fresher training), providing salient cues or prompts to ensure correct implementation of procedures (e.g., checklists), and providing consequential measures (e.g., feedback on correct and incorrect performance, reinforcing correct performance) are effective procedures.

In an example (DiGennaro-Reed, Codding, Catania, & Maguire, 2010) video modeling and performance feedback were used to increase teacher treatment integrity with respect to implementing behavior interventions for three teachers. Moreover, the teachers reported that they preferred the video modeling with performance feedback rather than just the video modeling. Interestingly, Noell, Lafleur, Mortenson, Ranier, and Levelle (2000) evaluated the effects of brief daily meetings and performance feedback to general education teachers' integrity of implementing peer tutoring interventions for reading. Only two of the teachers improved with the daily meetings, but all the teachers' integrity increased with the performance feedback. This study succinctly demonstrates the need for performance feedback (discussed in Chapter 6) for improved and maintained treatment fidelity.

SUMMARY AND CONCLUSIONS

To interpret the results of any intervention, it is necessary to record and report on how accurately the intervention was implemented; this is known as treatment integrity. Just like the first step in any measurement situation, the first step in assessing treatment integrity is to operationally define what is the correct and incorrect implementation of a procedure. One way to develop the operational definitions of what is correct and incorrect, and also a measurement tool, is to develop and use a task analysis to record information on treatment fidelity. Although recording data on treatment integrity is important in its own right, what is done with those data is even more important. In other words, just assessing behavior does not have a significant impact. Utilizing those assessment data to go forward is the real task. That is why it is important to follow up after the assessment and implement an intervention with the consultee if the assessment indicates treatment integrity failure.

ACTIVITIES

1. Operationally define correct and incorrect implementation for your consultee.
2. Develop a task analysis of the intervention and use it to determine treatment integrity by your consultee.
3. Describe what you could do about integrity failures.

Chapter 6

Promoting Continued Implementation

As you know, the best way to strengthen a behavior is to reinforce it. This, of course, holds true for consultees (the significant others implementing the intervention) as it does for clients (the person receiving the intervention). The previous two chapters have addressed various actions you can take to help promote program implementation with fidelity, and how to determine what level of fidelity has been achieved. Now, we address what can be done to help ensure continued program implementation beyond the first several days. As Sugai and Horner (1999) have said, "the real challenge is not identifying and developing new strategies, but in delivering and maintaining the strategies…" (p. 12). In this chapter we focus is on delivering interventions; in the next chapter, we will turn our attention to maintaining those interventions and behavior.

We have pointed out how constructive changes by consultees often require considerable effort on their part. It should come as no surprise, then, that a number of studies have reported that even though a newly implemented intervention brought about improvements in the targeted behavior(s), this consequence of client improvement alone did not result in the consultees' continued implementation of the program (e.g., Alvero et al., 2001; Anderson, Crowell, Sucec, Gilligan, & Wikoff, 1982; Coles & Blunden, 1981; Digennaro et al., 2007; Johnson & Katz, 1973; Loeber, 1971; MacDonald, Gallimore, & MacDonald, 1970; Montegar, Reid, Madsen, & Ewell, 1977; Rose & Church, 1998). For example, even though a program implemented in a hospital for individuals with mental handicaps resulted in marked increases in appropriate resident behavior with corresponding reductions in inappropriate behavior, this improvement did not result in the staff continuing to use these procedures during a six-month follow-up period until feedback was used with the staff members (Coles & Bluden, 1981). Similarly, even though a token-reinforcement program resulted in increases in client-contracting behavior by real-estate agents, removal of the program resulted in contacts reverting nearly to baseline levels even though the number of contacts were related to greater sales (Anderson et al., 1982). Further, after reviewing numerous studies which used parents as change agents for their children, Johnson and Katz concluded:

> It is generally assumed that parents are highly motivated to receive training in as much as they are the ones most directly affected (or punished) by their children's disruptive activity. However, many therapists have found it worthwhile to utilize extrinsic reinforces… to encourage parents working to change their children's activity as well as to maintain newly acquired management skills. (p. 189)

Other contingencies, in addition to client behavior improvement, appear to be necessary to help new consultee behavior patterns become established. Consultees usually will need frequent, direct assistance from you, the consultant, to establish new patterns of behavior.

Some time ago, Dustin (1974) pointed out the importance of ongoing supportive feedback. "It is necessary that a change agent possess tenacity to follow through and to return to the same tasks and the same individuals time and again" (p. 424). A lack of doing so explains the failure of many consultants who attempt to change consultees' behavior with infrequent visits or contacts. Too often after the intervention shows initial gains, it is often forgotten, inconsistently monitored and implemented, and data collection becomes more infrequent. This results in much initial effort wasted and behavioral changes that do not last.

PROVIDE FEEDBACK

Mayer et al. (2019) have defined feedback as:

> Information transmitted back to the responder following a particular performance in a form that may influence behavior: seeing or hearing about specific features of the results. Feedback may function as a reinforcer or punisher, and/or may serve as a discriminative function. Its form can vary too, from a subtle facial expression or gesture, to a set of general spoken comments (e.g., 'Nice job!' 'Good going!' 'That was awesome!') to precise quantitative measures (e.g., 'Your praise has increased from a baseline of about 3-times an hour to 6-times an hour').(p. 771)

Delivering feedback is one of the most useful and powerful management tools you can use within a commercial, educational, service organization, or a family, and it appears to be a primary factor for improving treatment integrity (Codding, Livanis, Pace, & Vaca, 2008). It consists of good operant conditioning procedures (Mangiapanello & Hemmes, 2015), and is a major component of behavioral skills training (see Chapter 4).

Conduct Feedback Sessions

A monitoring and feedback session should be systematically scheduled to ensure treatment fidelity (e.g., after initial competency is demonstrated, a bi-monthly, monthly, or quarterly schedule should be developed). It is important that monitoring of the intervention is consistently conducted to demonstrate continued effectiveness. Although the consultant will intially be the one to conduct these assessments and feedback sessions, a continued monitoring system should be developed either internally or with continued consultation.

Before we get into the specific details regarding the content and schedule of providing feedback, it might be worthwhile to go over the suggested steps regarding providing feedback. It is recommended that when providing feedback the following steps be adhered to: 1) provide an empathetic statement by paraphrasing what the consultee is experiencing; 2) describe the correct performance (see *Specific Feedback* section below as to how this should be stated); 3) identify incorrect performance (see *Use Specific Feedback* and *Dealing with Errors* sections below on how this should be stated); 4) describe how performance should occur (re-teach); 5) provide opportunities for questions; 6) inform about future monitoring; and 7) end the feedback session on a positive note (see box on a task analysis of this process).

Use Specific Feedback

Because our objective is to improve performance, make your feedback specific to the behavior and *be constructive and positive rather than vague or aversive*. Communicate and differentially reinforce what was done correctly (Steps 2 & 3). "Nice going! You not only complemented Jim's on-task behavior, but also Albert, as soon as he got back on-task." "Super, you waited a full ten seconds before providing that prompt. That takes a lot of patience, but you did it." Note how in both of these examples the consultee's behavior was defined objectively and a positive comment was made about the behavior. This makes it clear to the consultee the exact behavior to demonstrate.

It is also important to be specific regarding what was done incorrectly and what they should have done (Steps 3 & 4). As a consultant or manager, certainly you want to be welcomed as helpful, rather than be avoided as a threat. So, as we have said many times, try to *accentuate the positive whenever pos-*

> **Task Analysis for Providing Feedback**
>
> 1. Begin with empathetic and/or positive statement (e.g., " I know ignoring Johnny when he spits is really hard and it is gross when he spits in your face, but you are doing a great job of playing with him and presenting learning opportunities when he is not spitting).''
> 2. Describe correct performance (e.g., "When Johnny spits we want to make sure that we do not give him any attention. Remember, we identified that Johnny spits to get any kind of attention he can").
> 3. Identify incorrect performance and specify how performance should be carried out. Inform individual exactly how to improve performance and demonstrate correct implementation/performance (e.g., "When Johnny spits on you, just walk away. Don't say anything, don't shake your head or frown at him. Say 'pretend he just spit on me and watch what I do' while walking away in a natural manner"). It is a good idea to use BST at this step.
> 4. Provide opportunity for questions (e.g., "Does that make sense? Do you have any questions? Do you need anything to be able to do this?").
> 5. Inform about future monitoring (e.g., "Over the next three days I will be stopping by to observe your progress and provide you support in walking away from this bothersome behavior").
> 6. End the feedback session with a positive statement (e.g., "Thank you so much for being open to my feedback... you are doing a great job trying to do this program.... I'm so excited to see how Johnny's behavior will change").

sible, by providing more supportive (stressing what was done correctly) than corrective feedback (pointing out the errors that were made). When corrective feedback is necessary, use modeling and differential reinforcement to show the correct behavior, rather than making a punitive comment. "I see you are now recognizing Billy more when he is on-task and forgetting to withhold your attention when he is playing around only once in awhile. It's hard to change old behaviors, isn't it? Would it be helpful if we role-played some more examples?" Make sure to allow for the consultee to ask questions after you have provided feedback and ensure you end any feedback on a positive note so as to not make feedback aversive.

Use Various Forms of Feedback

Feedback can take various forms, and it is best to use more than one form of feedback. For example, feedback can be provided in person, by phone, email, written notes, graphed data paired with recognition and praise, complimentary notes with a copy to your consultee's supervisor or significant other, and, as illustrated above, with specific feedback and praise.

Enhance Feedback's Effectiveness

PROVIDE FREQUENT AND IMMEDIATE REINFORCEMENT. Feedback, when teaching your consultee a new skill, is more effective when it is provided frequently and immediately. For example, Petscher and Bailey (2006) observed that instructional assistants were not accurately implementing a token economy for which they had been trained. A brief follow-up in-service had no measurable effect on the accuracy of their implementation. Their accuracy of implementation only improved after they were provided with ongoing prompting, self-monitoring, and accuracy feedback. In another study (DiGennaro, Martens, & Kleinmann, 2007), the consultant continued to coach and provide immediate corrective feedback until each teacher implemented the plan with 100 percent accuracy on two consecutive occasions.

Often, feedback is provided a day or two later (Sweigart, Landrum, & Pennington, 2015). To correct such a situation, Sweigart and his colleagues wanted to immediately show a middle school resource math teacher how much positive feedback she was providing her students. To do so, they transferred the data from an Excel laptop workbook to an iPad that the teacher kept within view during each session. As a result, not only did her use of positive feedback increase, but her students' engagement increased and their disruptions decreased.

In an example in a southeastern United States food-service distributor warehouse, selection errors were reduced by using a voice-assisted selecting tool that provided immediate feedback when errors occurred (Berger & Ludwig, 2007). Selection errors reduced from 2.44 per 1,000 cases to 0.94.

To be an effective change agent, then, you must not only administer immediate feedback, but you also need to administer it frequently (Step 5). As Mayer et al. (2019) have pointed out, "Programs lacking ongoing feedback risk failure" (p. 533). Early studies pointed this fact out. For example, MacDonald et al (1970) noted that parents and relatives needed feedback with reinforcement in the form of face-to-face meetings or phone conversations at least twice a week for them to maintain behavioral contracts made with their adolescents for increasing school attendance. Similarly, Hunt and Sulzer-Azaroff (1974) helped parents to develop an intervention program tailored for their child. They then contacted half of the parents regularly twice a week. The other half were not contacted. Those who received the twice a week contact to answer questions and to provide praise for their efforts all went on to have success. Only 25 percent of those in the other group without the follow-up contact went on to have success. This also means that 75 percent likely experienced additional frustration and failure. Comparable studies with teachers (Holden & Sulzer-Azaroff, 1972) and staff in a residential care facility (Mozingo et al., 2006) reported similar results. Based on such studies, it would appear that *you need to provide feedback at least twice a week to help a consultee establish, or learn, a new skill*. If not, your consultee is likely to encounter frustration and failure, or punishment, in their attempts at implementing the intervention program. Such findings should come as no surprise. We all know that reinforcement is more effective when delivered immediately and frequently when establishing a behavior. Fortunately, once a new behavior is well established, feedback and reinforcement can be thinned gradually to weekly (Mortenson & Witt, 1998), biweekly (Codding, Feinberg Dunn, & Pace, 2005) and, even less frequently as the natural environment begins to support the behavior.

Related to immediacy, an immediate response to initial requests for assistance is important to those of you who are (or might be) working in an institutional setting. The person requesting help may soon stop asking for your assistance if you don't respond in a timely manner. Their requesting behavior may undergo extinction if reinforcement (i.e., your responding) is delayed for several weeks. Your assistance is more likely to be sought if you can respond to each request with a statement such as, "I can be in your ____ (class, home, office, etc.) during the next hour. Will that be convenient for you?" When you are unable to meet soon, at least set up an appointment immediately for the earliest date and time possible.

Immediate reinforcement also can be provided when the consultee observes rapid results from the intervention. When the consultee can see from a graph that the procedure is bringing about the desired change, they are, in essence, reinforced for their actions. Recognizing this effect of rapid results some time ago, early advocates of behavioral counseling suggested that you should initially help the consultee "select a specific workable behavior problem where results can be observable within a short period of time" (Krumboltz & Thoresen, 1969, p. 154). This strategy can help provide more immediate reinforcement for the consultee's behavior. Too often, consultees are encouraged or allowed to work on a difficult behavioral problem that can take too long to show results. Under such circumstances, reinforcement is delayed too long for the consultee's responding, resulting in a loss of treatment integrity. (A lack of results or failure acts as a punisher to the consultee's use of the behavioral approach and may impact the likelihood that the consultee will trust future recommendations.) Thus, particularly during your beginning consultation sessions, quick initial success should be provided for the consultee.

You will not, of course, always be able to jointly select a goal that will bring quick success. Furthermore, you will find that for some consultees, client improvement, as mentioned above, is not sufficiently reinforcing to maintain program implementation Because of this, we next discuss the importance of you using a variety of reinforcers, and the necessity of having others provide reinforcement for the consultee's program implementation.

USE A VARIETY OF REINFORCERS. As you are aware, if you use the same reinforcer over and over again, its effectiveness is likely to diminish. Generally, the greater the variety of reinforcers you use to directly reinforce the consultee's correct program implementation, the greater the likelihood of correct implementation. On page 83 we present Table 6.1 containing a listing of possible reinforcers that can be used with consultees. Some of these *potential* reinforcers are discussed in more detail in the rest of this chapter. Also, note that we refer to them as potential reinforcers. You will need to determine which might be reinforcing for each of the Consultees you work with by observing their effects on your consultee's behavior.

Some consultants have capitalized on the Premack Principle to help motivate consultees to implement a behavioral program. For example, a teacher, Mrs. Meyer, said, "I would like to use reinforcement more in my classroom but I never can find the time with so many students to teach. I can't even find the time to work on my lesson plans." The consultant knew that Mrs. Meyer spent a lot of her free time working on lesson plans and developing objectives. She had also reported that the she enjoyed planning activities. Thus, the consultant offered to take over her classroom for a short period of time so she could work on her classroom planning (a high frequency behavior) if she would use just five minutes at the beginning of individual reading time to reinforce the behavior of individual students (a low frequency behavior). She agreed. This was the start of Mrs. Meyer's increased, independent usage of positive reinforcement. Her students began to reinforce her compliments as she reinforced their appropriate behavior, and the consultant was able to gradually reduce his presence, and time spent teaching, in the classroom. The natural environment was now maintaining Mrs. Meyer's frequent use of reinforcement.

Sometimes you can also use **negative reinforcement** when working with a consultee. Negative reinforcement, as with positive reinforcement, can help establish you as a reinforcing agent. However, we do not recommend that you introduce an aversive to use negative reinforcement. If you administer aversives, your consultees are likely to respond by being aggressive (telling you where to go), turning their backs, or by leaving (escaping) whenever you show up.

As Mayer and McGookin (1977) pointed out, some professionals argue that when consultees have had a particularly trying day with their client(s), they need a chance to unwind and purge themselves of the tension built up during the day. If it is true that a consultee is experiencing an aversive state (anxiety, anger, etc.) and that talking to another about it helps to relieve this aversive state, then this would be a way to establish yourself as a reinforcing agent through negative reinforcement. Listening also provides you the opportunity to help more concretely. You might hear information that can be used to assist your consultee in improving the situation. However, some consultees have been known to, or taught to, use consultants as "crying towels" rather than as sources of assistance. As Brown (1974) pointed out some time ago: "Attention should be given to bolstering adequate performance, not inefficiency" (p. 196).

You also can attempt to remove aversives already present in the consultee's environment, as illustrated in the following example. An administrator requested help with a teacher whose classroom students were "out of control." The teacher had been informed by the administrator that if she was not able get gain control

Table 6.1 Possible Reinforcers for the Behavior of Program Implementers

Praise

Praise from 　clients 　supervisors 　parents 　peers Public compliments (e.g., in newsletter, over P.A. system)	Complimenting client(s) in the presence of program implementer Specific or labeled praise Positive feedback to one another Gestures: smiles, nods, etc.

Written Congratulatory Feedback

Individualized positive notes from client, parents, behavior analyst, etc. Appreciative letters with copies sent to supervisor Positive notes in personnel file	Thank-you's in daily bulletin or newsletter Compliments on specific bulletin boards Spotlight program implementer in newspaper

Tangible Rewards

Buttons Lunch at supervisor's expense Choice of restaurant Food/treats Bonus money, or voucher, for special supplies or equipment Cash award X gallons of gasoline	Tickets to theater, sporting, musical events Certificates Special lunches/dinners Small gifts Bonus supplies or equipment Merit raise Supermarket shopping spree

Miscellaneous

Release from extra duties Early release from work Immediate response to request for help Phone calls expressing appreciation or recognition Cited *Program Implementer of the Month*	Release/paid time for attending in-service training or workshops Supervisor, behavior analyst, others listening to concerns and providing assistance Redecorating staff meeting or lounge room

*This table is a modification of one from Mayer & Ybarra (2003)

of her class, she would be let go, and a note was placed in her file pointing out her lack of classroom control. The consultant got the administrator to agree to remove the note if the teacher got the situation turned around. The negative reinforcer in this situation was the removal of the damaging note in the teacher's personnel file. Classroom behavior, with the help of the consultant, was turned around, the note removed from her file, and she did not lose her job. Another example of using negative reinforcement is when the consultant is able to work out a program with the consultee that quickly stops a client from misbehaving. As you remove aversives, you begin to establish yourself as a reinforcing agent, and an individual who can be of assistance. However, be sure to rely on providing positive reinforcers. They are usually more available and can produce a variety of behavior changes.

USE MODELING AS AN ERROR CORRECTION PROCEDURE. Modeling has been successfully used to help correct errors. This **error correction procedure** consists of you modeling the correct response after the behavior interventionist makes an error, and then encourage him or her to imitate the behavior you modeled. Then, of course, be sure to reinforce correct imitation. This type of error correction procedure appears better than making a punitive comment such as, "No, that's incorrect." It is minimally intrusive and has been found to be an especially effective way to correct most errors (Barbetta, Heron, & Heward, 1993; Carroll, Owsiany, & Cheatham, 2018; Kodak et al., 2016; McGhan & Lerman, 2013). Also, it is easier to imitate a modeled behavior than it is to follow instructions.

USE DIFFERENTIAL REINFORCEMENT PROCEDURES. Don't forget to use differential reinforcement procedures to decrease errors and help clarify the differences between correct and incorrect implementation, such as Differential Reinforcement of Alternative Behaviors (DRA), Differential Reinforcement of Diminishing Rates (DRD) and Differential Reinforcement of Other Behaviors (DRO). Following modeling, be sure to differentially reinforce the occurrence of appropriate interventions (DRA). These combined procedures will help teach the consultee the correct intervention to use. In addition, you can recognize and reinforce reduced rates (DRD) and periods of non-occurrence (DRO) of errors. By using modeling and these differential reinforcement strategies, you increase the reinforcement delivered to the implementer's correct application of the intervention, and you can achieve a more rapid reduction in errors.

Here is an example: A consultee was observed by the behavioral consultant to frequently point out errors by saying, "that's wrong." The consultee would also use the same praise statement over and over: "I like the way you _____" in a monotone voice. The consultant modeled for him how he, the consultee, could use modeling in place of saying "that's wrong" and they role-played the skill. On subsequent visits the consultant differentially reinforced instances in which modeling was used. The consultant did, however, point out and reinforce periods of time during which "That's wrong." was not used (DRO), and also reinforced when criticism was used less frequently during other periods of time (DRD). He also observed that the consultee patted a client on the back so the consultant said, "I noticed you use a variety of reinforcers in your class. You patted John on the back for his performance and praised him earlier for being on task. That's very important. Some people just use the same reinforces or comment over and over again, and it loses its effect. The client eventually tuned them out. I'm glad to see that you are using a variety." At each subsequent observation the consultant verbally reinforced the consultee for using a variety of different reinforces, always stressing the positive, and tying these changes into student changes. Soon the consultant showed the consultee a graph depicting that the consultee was even increasing his use of different reinforcers. The program was successful. Of course, the consultant was careful to use a variety of reinforcers with the consultee as he was teaching him to do with his client.

PROVIDE A RATIONALE FOR PROGRAM IMPLEMENTATION. Research related to modeling has shown that behavior interventionists are more likely to imitate what is modeled, generalize the skill, and retain it when they understand the reasons, or rationale for the intervention (Boyce & Geller, 2001; Braukmann, Maloney, Fixsen, Phillips, & Wolf, 1974; Poche, Brouwer & Swearingen, 1981; Zimmerman & Rosenthal, 1974). For example, when using modeling, you will probably suggest using multiple models. When you do, point out the reason for doing so: (1) Several models exert more influence than a single model (Barton & Bevirt, 1981; DeRicco & Niemann, 1980); and (2) Selecting the same peer or person as a model often causes them to be labeled as supervisor's favorite," or as the "teacher's pet" in a classroom, and sometimes to be ostracized by the group.

PROVIDE FOR PROBLEM-SOLVING AS NECESSARY. Investigators (Minor, DuBardk, & Luiselli, 2014) found that neither correction, praise, nor feedback successfully promoted teachers' rates of implementing behavior intervention programs. However, once they added problem-solving in the form of discussing potential barriers to implementation, how to overcome those, and jointly addressed procedural modifications to correct procedural misapplications, uniform improvement resulted. Thus, when sufficient progress is not being made, consider taking time to jointly problem-solve.

ENSURE ENVIRONMENTAL SUPPORT AND REINFORCEMENT

If the natural environment does not provide support or reinforcement for program implementation, the consultee will not continue to implement the program. As Mayer et al. (2019) point out: "Identifying and using a variety of reinforcing sources to support and maintain program implementation efforts become especially critical as you gradually begin to withdraw your support" (p. 543). You need to involve other willing participants, such as supervisors, peers, clients, consumers, parents, other professionals, and other family members, colleagues, or friends. *Do not depend on your own prompts and reinforcers to sustain par-*

ent, teacher, staff or employee program implementation. Involve key people in supporting program implementation.* By involving key people, (1) the natural social environment can begin to serve as a source of prompting and reinforcing program implementation in your absence; and (2) it allows you gradually to fade your prompting and thin your reinforcer delivery as the natural environment begins to maintain program implementation. As investigators (Boyce & Geller, 2001) point out, targeted behaviors are more likely to sustain when supported by those normally present. Also, people who experience support from their peers and colleagues are less likely to report burnout (Corrigan et al., 1998). Thus, let's look at who might be key people you can involve in supporting program implementation.

Peers

Do not overlook peer influences. Peers can serve as models and they can reinforce instances of program implementation by providing recognition, compliments, materials, and suggestions. For example, four typically developing preschool students were taught to attend to their teachers when their individual names were called and when the class was asked to pay attention (Beaulien, et al., 2013). However, these responses did not maintain until classroom peers were taught to remind and praise one another for attending.

Teams within schools and other organizations have been shown to promote peer cooperation, positive programming, and staff retention while alleviating stress and reducing burnout (Corrigan, et al., 1998; Gersten, Keating, Yovanoff, & Harniss, 2001; Whitaker, 2000). Consider doing the following:

- Encourage consultees to meet with one another to discuss various procedures they have found helpful in serving their clients. (School personnel were found to be more accepting of interventions developed by a team that included teachers and a behavior expert than a plan developed solely by an expert) (Crone, Hawken, & Bergstrom, 2007).
- Encourage consultees to observe specific (model) programs that their peers are implementing.
- Let consultees know when their colleagues need help.
- Assist and reinforce peers or colleagues for offering to help one another, complimenting one another's program implementation, and for communicating appreciation to one another.
- Encourage others in the organization or home to provide reinforcers for program implementation.

In the home, encourage the spouse, domestic partner, friends, relatives, neighbors, and others to regularly recognize the efforts in implementing the program by parents. (Recall the influence of significant others as pointed out in Chapter 1.) Similarly, expressions of appreciation and cooperation from parents to others working with their child, such as teachers, counselors, speech and language professional, or psychologists, can function as powerful reinforcers to continue their assistance. Therefore, keep parents regularly informed about what is happening and how this is helping their child. Encourage parents to let service providers know how much they appreciate what they are doing to help their child. And, of course, encourage those who have influence with the parent(s), serving as interventionists, to recognize the parents' efforts in helping their child.

In organizations, encourage other managers or supervisors, directors, and even CEOs to regularly recognize the efforts of the consultee implementing the program. Create a team of managers who can reinforce each other for implementing procedures with their supervisees.

Clients

Clients can serve as sources of reinforcement for program implementation. The reinforcers derive not only from evidence of their progress, but also from their positive comments, smiles, compliments, and so on, directed toward the consultee. In classic studies (Graubard et al., 1971; Sherman & Cormier, 1974), twelve 15-year-olds were taught to increase their teachers' rates of praise and to decrease negative comments and punishment by using the following techniques: (1) contingent compliments (e.g., "Gee, it makes me feel good and I work better when you praise me"; "I like the way you teach this lesson"); (2) asking for extra assignments; and (3) contingent non-vocal behaviors (e.g., making eye contact, sitting up straight, and nodding in agreement as their teacher spoke). They also learned to look down and remain quiet while receiving any negative comments or punishers from their teacher. Within a short time, these strategies were effective in that the teacher dramatically increased her use of praise and diminished her disapproving comments. Also, the students reported how much nicer their teachers had become; the teachers reported how much more mature their students seemed to be. A similar strategy was used (Craft, Alber, & Heward, 1998) when teaching fourth graders with developmental disabilities to recruit teacher attention while they worked on spelling assignments in their regular education classroom. Not only did teacher attention statements increase in the regular classroom, but so did teacher praise received by these students, their percentage of worksheet items completed, and their accuracy on spelling assignments. Clients, then, offer a powerful, inexpensive, and natural source of reinforcement that you can use to the benefit of all involved. Think about how natural and cost-effective it would be to get employees to reinforce their supervisors for using positive-based interventions to manage their behavior.

Parents

Parents can be a powerful source of reinforcement. You should capitalize on and use this source whenever possible. You can point out to parents what the RBT is doing and has accomplished and suggest that they express their appreciation to the RBT. Similarly, you can point out what others (teachers and various specialists) have done or are doing and stress the importance of their expressing their appreciation. Specifics would be reinforced whenever possible. For example, when parents note that their son comes home excited because he received a "happy face" or a positive comment from his teacher on his paper, encourage the parents to let the teacher know not only how much the child appreciates it, but that the parents also appreciate it. Such expressions by the parents will enhance the likelihood that the RBT and teacher will continue to implement the behavioral programs as part of their regular routine. Plus, they are likely to enhance the enjoyment they get from their work.

Supervisors, Managers, Administrators

Because supervisors, managers, and administrators are chiefly responsible for seeing to it that their employees do a good job, programmatic success depends on how effectively they support and assist their employees. By their very nature, those positions typically entitle them to initiate particular reinforcing and perhaps disciplinary actions. Depending on the character of the organization, these could affect decisions related to job assignments, hiring and firing, setting wages, awarding salary increases, expressing approval, dispensing privileges, scheduling breaks and vacation, recommending promotions and/or tenure, and assigning and maintaining quality assurance over tasks or products.

The extent to which staff involved in a behavior change program cooperate and/or experience stress depends in good part on the nature of the supervisor support they receive. Such factors can even influence personnel to decide whether or not to remain on the job (Brunsting, Sreckovic, & Lane, 2014; Cancio, Albrecht, & Johns, 2013; Gersten et al., 2001). When special education teachers reported experiencing appreciation, opportunities for growth, and trust from their supervisors, they were more likely to express an intent to remain in the field (Cancio et al., 2013). Clear administrative direction and support also serve to counteract teacher burnout (Brunsting et al., 2014).

According to Gallessich (1973), the principal is usually the most influential person in the school. Their "educational orientation, administrative style, decision-making patterns and relations with central administration, faculty, and community affect all aspects of the school" (p. 60). Support for this conclusion derives from an intervention designed to reduce school vandalism. Vandalism rates and costs decreased in schools in which the administrators were seen by personnel to be high involved and supportive in the intervention programs, while in schools with less involved administrators, vandalism costs continued to increase (Mayer, Butterworth, Komoto, & Benoit, 1983). Similarly, McIntosh et al. (2014) found that along with team functioning, teachers rated administrative support as the most important feature for both school-wide program implementation and sustainability.

In another study (Gillat & Sulzer-Azaroff, 1994), the senior investigator taught school principals specific skills in time management, goal-setting, praising, and non-vocal approval (e.g., head nods, smiles). Principals then scheduled a few minutes a week to visit the classrooms, review wall charts displaying student performance, and compliment both student and teachers on the students' progress. Grade-school students memorized their multiplication tables much more quickly and middle-school students independently read substantially more pages as a function of those increases in positive attention. Similarly, a study by Cossairt et al. (1973) found that student progress alone was not sufficient to increase teachers' use of praise, but when the principals intermittently complimented them when they did praise, those rates maintained and even increased further.

Another example was set in a residential care facility (Mozingo et al., 2006). The experimenters evaluated the impact of a staff training and management package designed to increase frequency of accurate recording of problem behavior. Following in-service training, only two of eight participants increased their accuracy, but when the supervisor was present and provided support and feedback, all eight improved. On achieving parallel results, Cooper (2006) concluded that "management's demonstrable support was significantly associated with behavioral safety performance" (p. 1).

Mayer et al. (2019) provide the following examples of ways that supervisors, managers, and administrators can display active or demonstrable support:

- Positively recognize personnel who implement programs as planned.
- Be present at behavior support team meetings.
- Provide resources.
- Release personnel from their assigned work to train, assist, and observe other program implementers.
- Aid in establishing needed policy and community contacts.
- Compensate staff involvement in committee work and training by subtracting other duties or responsibilities.
- Recognize client improvements.

Other Possible Reinforcing Sources or Activities

VISITORS. Compliments on the consultee's work and the client's progress from visitors can be very reinforcing to continued program implementation. Visitors to homes, classrooms and other institutional and work settings can include counselors, school psychologists, administrators/supervisors, resource and department heads, parents, peers, etc. Discuss and point out to them the effects of the consultee's programs on their clients or employees. (e.g., "Look how well she uses positive control with her clients." "She sure gives her clients credit when credit is due." "Mrs. Smith has one of the best classrooms I have ever seen.") Encourage them to relay to the consultee their appreciation and impressions.

RELEASED TIME WITH PAY. Consultees can learn from one another. If possible, arrange for someone to take over the consultee's responsibilities, or excuse the consultee from them for a brief period during which he or she can visit and observe model programs that other consultees are implementing.

RESOURCES. Suggest and provide resources as appropriate. Help make initial contacts to collaborate with other professionals (e.g., doctors, speech and language specialists) as needed. Above all, make yourself available and easily accessible.

PROFESSIONAL RECOGNITION. When appropriate and if possible, involve the consultees in professional presentations, conference attendance, and model certain behavioral programs for other consultees. Placing them in the limelight often offers many consultees additional reinforcement. However, like any potential reinforcer, check out its reinforcing potential before using it on the consultee's behavior. Some consultees become very uneasy when they have to perform in front of or speak to a group of other professionals. Therefore, use of this potential reinforcing activity must be decided upon carefully. For some consultees it could prove very punishing.

CAUTION. Be sure to observe the effects of any potential reinforcers you select, for as mentioned in Chapter 4, if your reinforcer selection is incorrect it can damage not only the effectiveness of the intervention but also the relationship you have with your consultee.

SUMMARY AND CONCLUSIONS

Reinforcement with consultees follow the same basic guides as when used with clients. You should not rely solely on client progress and the feedback you provide. Client progress and your feedback are critically important, but a key to successful consulting is arranging the natural environment so that your consultees will receive a variety of reinforcers from differing existing sources. Lasting behavior change, including program implementation, is much more likely when supported by various sources in the natural environment. Furthermore, the effects of your consulting interventions must be constantly monitored to ensure that the desired effects are occurring. If not, you must alter the program (as you would do with a client if the program was not producing the desired results).

ACTIVITIES

1. Describe how to (a) provide feedback and (b) what you can do to enhance your feedback's effectiveness.
2. Describe what you can do to enhance environmental support for your consultee, and specify why it is so important that you promote environmental support.

Chapter 7

Helping Consultees "Make It on Their Own"

Maintenance and Generalization

Mobilizing the environment was discussed in the previous chapter as a means of helping your consultees function effectively in your absence. We now turn our attention to additional methods you can use to help consultees "make it on their own." These include reducing prompts and reinforcers.

REDUCING PROMPTS

Care must be taken to avoid overuse of artificial prompts (those not occurring naturally in the environment, such as repeated reminders and demonstrations) and to gradually fade those that are used. The task itself should become the natural prompt. An overuse of prompts can lead to an over-dependence on your assistance by some consultees, and to resentment by others. As Krumboltz and Krumboltz (1972) noted a number of years ago, "Even under the best circumstances most people do not like to depend on others to give them cues. They want to be independent and will readily interpret someone else's deliberate cue as an effort to control" (p. 76). You need to be particularly sensitive to any environmental cues that might signal an over- or under-use of prompts. Reminder phone calls made too often can turn off a consultee. Rather than serving as helpful prompts, too-frequent phone calls can become an annoyance or a punisher. Similarly, too many reminders to a consultee can be irritating. It is necessary to reduce the frequency of delivering prompts as soon as the consultee is observed to be applying the strategy consistently. The sooner your artificial prompts are removed, the sooner the consultees are able to help the client without overly depending on you, the consultant. And, most importantly, the sooner consultees are able to maintain strategies by themselves, the sooner they are likely to regard such strategies as their own and use them with feelings of pride and ownership. Hence, a delay in withdrawing prompts could rob the consultee of that belief.

Please do not infer from the above discussion that prompts should be abruptly withdrawn. You must be careful to avoid sudden reductions in prompts that have been provided to help the consultee implement the strategy. Should the consultee begin to falter in implementing the intervention, the reduction in prompts likely has been too abrupt. A return to a more frequent use of prompts is then indicated. As your consultees acquire the skill of specifying goals, you *gradually* fade out your usage of questions, such as, "What do you want him to do?" Similarly, the activity of pointing out similarities between two situations to foster generalization is used less frequently as your consultees acquire proficient use of the procedures. As consultees acquire proficiency in using appropriate interventions, you gradually, not abruptly, fade out your directions, role playing (modeling), and other prompts. The consultee's behavior, then, gradually becomes less and less dependent upon your prompts. For example, Ringer (1973) gradually faded out his suggestions and modeling of a classroom token reinforcement program until he was able to completely withdraw his presence from the classroom. Further, as in Ringer's study, your use of fading is facilitated when it is made clear from the beginning that your initial participation, such as conducting part of the program, is *temporary*. Clearly, it should not be communicated that any part of the program is your responsibility and another part is the consultee's. Rather, convey that whatever responsibility you assume will be transferred over to the consultee as soon as possible.

REDUCING REINFORCERS

Once your consultee has attained the behavioral objective of successfully implementing the strategy, your next task is to help your consultee maintain the strategy without your support. The goal, then, is to help the consultee function effectively and independently without you. To achieve this goal, you fade both your use of prompts and gradually reduce your delivery of reinforcers.

As you know, to promote a behavior's increase to some desired level of occurrence, the best procedure is to reinforce the new behavior as often as it occurs. Reinforcing a behavior each time it occurs initially can minimize confusion and clarify what behavior must occur to receive reinforcement. Then, once the new behavior has been established, the reinforcers should be thinned gradually. Reinforcers should not be terminated abruptly. If abrupt termination of reinforcers does occur, the consultee is not likely to continue implementing the intervention.

When reducing the delivery of reinforcers, the consultant must always be sensitive to the consultee's behavior. As we have pointed out previously, engaging in new behavior is awkward and difficult for most people. Considerable reinforcement is necessary to maintain such behavior during its early phases. Also, sometimes a behavior change by the client appears obvious to the consultant, but not to the consultee. Thus, if your consultee begins to flounder when using a new strategy, you should realize that a more frequent delivery of reinforcers must be reinstated immediately if the consultee's use of the intervention is to be strengthened (or, alternatively, evidence of difficulty in implementing an intervention may signal the need to renegotiate your joint objectives for the client's behavior).

Once the behavior has been reestablished, the reinforcement can be reduced more gradually. For example, once it has become apparent to the consultee that the intervention being used is effectively reducing the disruptive behavior, your use of praise, phone calls, charts, and graphs can be reduced gradually until such reinforcement is no longer needed. What is influencing the consultee's behavior, then, is gradually shifted from the prompts and reinforcers provided by you to those provided by the natural environment.

What are the contingencies in the natural environment? Remember, you have succeeded in helping others to recognize and reinforce the consultee's implementation of the new intervention. By doing so, you are transferring stimulus control from you for prompting intervention use to the natural environment. Because others in the natural environment are beginning to become discriminative stimuli for implementing the intervention, your prompts and reinforcers become less and less necessary, helping the consultee to function more effectively and independently of you. You also increase the likelihood that the natural environment will continue to provide sporadic reinforcement over time.

Other advantages of reducing the frequent delivery of reinforcers are that it reduces the amount of time you must spend with any one consultee. Furthermore, it reduces the likelihood that too much reinforcement will be delivered by you, resulting in it becoming ineffective or irritating to the consultee. Reducing reinforcement also helps in other ways, as Cossairt, Hall and Hopkins (1973, p. 100) concluded in their study with teachers, though the findings appear applicable to most any consultee:

> Teacher praise maintained and even increased when teachers were placed on an intermittent schedule of social praise. This would seem to indicate that the excuse that principals and supportive staff do not have time for the social reinforcement of teacher behavior is invalid. Operant principles of reinforcement systematically applied would therefore seem to be functional in helping principals and consultants accomplish their primary goal, which should be improving instruction. It would also seem that this could be done with minimal amounts of time and effort.

Thinning of reinforcement to intermittent schedules, then, like the fading of prompts, assists consultants in achieving specified goals for their consultees, such as the increased use of positive reinforcement independently of consultants. Ideally, consultees should eventually be able to specify their own goals and effectively use intervention procedures without your assistance. Fading and thinning reinforcers are used by consultants to help promote such proficiency.

As the consultee becomes proficient in implementing interventions, you may observe that the program implementation is limited to a single client or situation. At such a point, you will need to turn to methods for helping your consultee generalize skills learned thus far to new targets for change.

PROMOTING GENERALIZATION

When helping consultees to begin using a new intervention, a segment of the day is often focused on making the task a bit easier. As your consultees become proficient in implementing the intervention during that time segment, it becomes important to help them to use it with the client in other time segments and in different situations. It also is important to help them to use the intervention with other clients for which it might be applicable. Your consultees have not met their objective of effectively using the intervention strategy until such on-going generalization occurs in your absence.

To help promote generalization, convey the expectation from the very beginning that the particular skills and procedures used during one segment of the day will be used during a variety times and situations and with other clients who might also profit from their use. To further promote their use with other clients, *point out the similarities* existing between the referred client and others having similar characteristics and problems. Point out the commonalities between the two situations. Similarities and commonalities between situations often function as prompts that will foster generalization. For example, it might be pointed out that two clients in the same situation have similar interests, hobbies, and share the common problem of low rates of remaining on-task. Occasionally, you might see an additional client whose needs are so similar to the target client to permit an easy transition of certain elements of the intervention to the second client. When this occurs, a nominal amount of time and effort can bring the second client into the intervention. In this way the consultee can discover the ease with which programs can be extended to others.

As you recall from your training in ABA, there are a number of other methods that also can be used to promote generalization. These include, but are not limited to: requesting the consultee to start using the intervention in other situations, times of day, and with other clients; training to fluency; continuing training the intervention in other environments; having the consultee record instances of using the intervention in other situations and with other clients, and noting what variations were used.

MAJOR POINTS FOR PROMOTING GENERALIZATION AND MAINTENANCE

Here are some general suggestions for promoting generalization and maintenance:

- Try to keep the training conditions as similar as possible to the natural setting, or gradually increase the similarity between the two. When possible, teach the skills in the environment where it is to be practiced.
- Teach consultees to record and evaluate their own behavior.
- Provide practice of the skill in a variety of settings.
- Teach consultees to reinforce their own behavior.
- Encourage those in the natural environment to reinforce the consultee's newly learned behaviors.
- Gradually withdraw your instructions, modeling, and other prompts as fluency begins to become established.
- Gradually withdraw your reinforces as the natural environment begins to assume contingency control (i.e., others in the environment begin to reinforce the behavior; results are obvious to the consultee).

SUMMARY AND CONCLUSIONS

The goal of all consultation is the maintenance and generalization of behavior change. As with any behavioral intervention, it is important to plan for maintenance and generalization from the beginning. As such is it important to move from continuous reinforcement schedules for less discriminable, intermittent, and natural reinforcers as well as incorporating various generalization strategies during consultation with the consultee. "Train and hope" should not be your consultation strategy with respect to your consultation approach.

ACTIVITIES

1. Describe how you will reduce your consultee's prompts and reinforcers.
2. Also describe how you will promote (a) generalization and (b) maintenance for your consultee.

Chapter 8

Assessing Consultation Effectiveness

As with any applied behavior analysis endeavor, assessing behavioral change is not only a cogent exercise, but a necessary requirement (Baer, Wolf, & Risley, 1968). In consultation services, it is necessary to not only measure the client's and consultee's performance, but to measure the consultant's behavior as well. In fact, a successful and effective consultation is achieved only when there are improvements at all three levels (you might say the process is effective when you achieve a trifecta). In behavioral consultation we address this issue by collecting measurement on the process of consultation as well as the outcomes of your consultation with both the consultee and the client.

MEASURING AT THE CLIENT LEVEL

Given that applied behavior analysis depends on demonstrating predictable and replicable improvements in socially significant behavior, it is no wonder that the first level of assessing the effectiveness of the consultation process is at the client level. If the consultation process is to be deemed successful, the behavior of the client must improve. Measuring client outcomes within a consultation relationship, however, is no different than utilizing objective, reliable, valid, and sensitive measures to demonstrate improvements in typical service delivery. In other words, to demonstrate effective consultation, there must be an improvement in the client's behavior as demonstrated by showing improvements utilizing either permanent product or process measures. Given this is standard practice in behavioral services, this book will not cover this material. With that said, there are ways of measuring client behaviors during consultation that vary somewhat from the standard ways of measuring individual client behaviors.

Sometimes during consultation at the system level, it is beneficial to measure group performance (i.e., the collection of clients). For example, if the consultation is occurring at a school district level, it would be important to not only measure improvements at an individual student level, but also to demonstrate improvements across a group of students (e.g., within a grade, local school, or across the whole district). Although the actual measurement procedures would be the same (e.g., number of behaviors, percentage of days, etc.), the summary and analysis would have an additional level of examination (i.e., the group level). Sheridan and colleagues (2017) evaluated the effects of consultation in rural schools by reporting outcome measures of students' positive and negative behaviors as means across students and during different times (e.g., baseline and intervention) to demonstrate effective consultation. In addition to reporting the behavioral data and utilizing visual inspection, the authors also tested the statistical significance of the obtained change across the school district. Similarly, an earlier study by Mayer et al. (1983) provided workshops and behavioral consultation to eighteen elementary and junior high schools over a three-year period to help develop more positive classrooms. They reported significant decreases in school-wide vandalism costs, and the rates of off-task behavior by students decreased significantly. In a similar study using behavioral consultation to produce more positive classrooms (Mayer, 1993), 200 9th grade high school students who were frequently absent (about 23 percent of the time) and had low grade point averages (1.31, about a D+) were followed from their 9th grade to the end of their 11th grade. By the end of the study, their dropout rates were lower than the overall district's dropout rate, and a 35.5 percent decrease in suspensions occurred. For more information on developing positive classrooms, see Mayer (2020).

ProtoFab Performance Improvement Project

A colleague who utilized many aspects of the consultation process described within this text provided us with permission to utilize a consultation project as an example to demonstrate a real life example of measurement at the client level. Sarah Arlington, M.S., BCBA, provided behavioral consultation to a millwright contractor and fabrication facility in Reno, Nevada (ProtoFab Inc.). The consultation team consisted of one BACB, two business owners, and five upper-level managers. The "clients" were 10 employees. The consultant established rapport by utilizing the *Professional Communication Skills* during a number of initial consultation meetings to better understand the work environment, the expectations of the owners regarding senior leaders and employees, and the expectations of the senior leaders about the management and employees. Initially, the owners sought to target employee retention;

however, after discussing that retention can be viewed as an outcome of other organization variables, the team choose to target performance targets (on-time arrival, clean work stations, and clean work trucks). Moreover, the team agreed to incorporate a differential reinforcement (with an added interdependent group contingency for two of the performance targets, clean work station and work truck) and feedback to increase these targets (specifics of the intervention can be obtained by contacting Sarah Arlington at sarahc43@gmail.com). It should be noted that the consultant had to spend some time understanding and overcoming the resistance of the team to use a reinforcement-based intervention, when the employees' "should just get to work on time and have a clean work station and truck." Intervention data were collected by two upper level managers and were analyzed by the organizational behavior management (OBM) consultant on a weekly basis and discussed in telephone meetings. The measurement system selected was percentage of completion for clean work trucks and clean workstations and percentage of on-time arrivals. On-time arrival data were 0% in baseline and averaged 78% for treatment package A and 91.6% for treatment package B. Clean work truck data were 0% for baseline and averaged 4% in package A and 80.6 percent in package B. Clean workstation data were 0% for baseline and averaged 5.3% in package A and 87.2% in package B (See Figure 8.1).

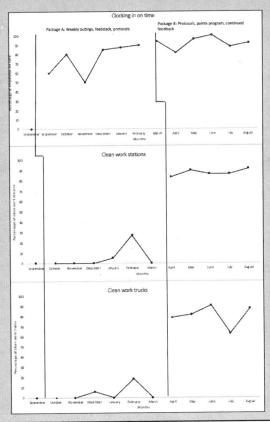

Figure 8.1

MEASURING AT THE CONSULTEE LEVEL

When evaluating the effects of any consultation relationship, the second level of assessment occurs with the consultee. We know that for any behavioral intervention to be effective, it needs to be implemented with integrity. Research has demonstrated that slight variations in treatment implementation can be costly with respect to client improvements. Because of the cogency of ensuring treatment fidelity and routinely assessing for treatment integrity, there are two chapters in this book devoted to this process (Chapters 4 & 5). Given the importance of treatment integrity, let's look at it in a little more detail. Sanetti and Kratohwill (2007) provide an overview of the research as it pertains to treatment integrity and consultation. They present the argument that consultants should not take a one-dimensional approach to treatment integrity. In fact, they suggested that besides measuring percentage of adherence to treatment protocols, that exposure and quality of delivery be measured as well. Thus, it is important when looking at the consultee's behavior to take into consideration the amount of consultation provided. For example, one could possibly argue that one two-hour consultation will have little effect on the consultee's behavior when compared to monthly two-hour consultation sessions across an academic year. Treatment drift of intervention procedures that were once implemented correctly can occur naturally over time. Therefore, frequent, consistent, and systematic measurements of program integrity is vital to the success of the program. Similarly, the quality of delivery has enormous effects on the outcomes of consultation. Although ensuring treatment fidelity is important, it is not the only measure related to the consultee. Because consultation is a relationship between the consultant and the consultee, it is important to measure that relationship.

Social validity refers to the acceptability of the goals, procedures, and outcomes. It is important to measure the social validity of one's consultation as a means for measuring an important outcome of consultation. Indeed, one way to measure the outcome of consultation is to demonstrate positive effects in the consultee's behavior and the client's behavior; however, the consultee's satisfaction of the consultant's behavior and intervention programs is equally important. Kratochwill, Elliot, and Busse (1995) provide a detailed example of how one might go about measuring the satisfaction of consultative performance. They conducted an indirect assessment to measure the consultee's satisfaction with the consultant's performance. The consultant evaluation assessment included a Likert-type scale questionnaire geared at evaluating the consultee's opinion on: general helpfulness; the usefulness of the information provided; the development of similar goals; listening skills; ability to identify resources; environmental fit; collaborative nature of relationship; ability to discuss identified problem; ability to assist without taking over; and likelihood of future request for consultation. In a more recent study, Kaiser, Rosenfield, and Gravois (2009) assessed consultees' (teachers') perception of satisfaction, skill development, and skill application as a means of determining social effectiveness of consultation. To provide a useful example of a social validity measure, we have developed a possible measure (however, it should be pointed out that this social validity measure has not be experimentally validated and should be used with caution).

Please answer the following questions regarding your consultant and the consultation experience.

1) The consultant was respectful and open to feedback throughout the consultation process.

   STRONGLY AGREE   AGREE   NEUTRAL   DISAGREE   STRONGLY DISAGREE

2) The consultant was a good listener.

   STRONGLY AGREE   AGREE   NEUTRAL   DISAGREE   STRONGLY DISAGREE

3) The consultant identified and provided useful resources.

   STRONGLY AGREE   AGREE   NEUTRAL   DISAGREE   STRONGLY DISAGREE

4) The consultant was collaborative rather than authoritarian.

   STRONGLY AGREE   AGREE   NEUTRAL   DISAGREE   STRONGLY DISAGREE

5) The consultant offered assistance rather than taking over.

   STRONGLY AGREE   AGREE   NEUTRAL   DISAGREE   STRONGLY DISAGREE

6) The consultant provided justification regarding all procedures and interventions.

   STRONGLY AGREE   AGREE   NEUTRAL   DISAGREE   STRONGLY DISAGREE

7) The consultant provided constructive feedback in an empathetic way.

   STRONGLY AGREE   AGREE   NEUTRAL   DISAGREE   STRONGLY DISAGREE

8) The consultant modeled all procedures until I felt comfortable prior to having me implement procedures with the client.

   STRONGLY AGREE   AGREE   NEUTRAL   DISAGREE   STRONGLY DISAGREE

9) The consultant and I role played what was modeled until I felt comfortable prior to having me implement the procedure on my own

   STRONGLY AGREE   AGREE   NEUTRAL   DISAGREE   STRONGLY DISAGREE

10) I felt like I could ask the consultant anything and that I would be heard.

    STRONGLY AGREE   AGREE   NEUTRAL   DISAGREE   STRONGLY DISAGREE

11) I was satisfied with the consultation process.

    STRONGLY AGREE   AGREE   NEUTRAL   DISAGREE   STRONGLY DISAGREE

12) I would recommend the consultant to others.

    STRONGLY AGREE   AGREE   NEUTRAL   DISAGREE   STRONGLY DISAGREE

13) I would reach out to the consultant in the future.

    STRONGLY AGREE   AGREE   NEUTRAL   DISAGREE   STRONGLY DISAGREE

14) I believe the consultant heard my concerns and addressed them in a professional manner.

    STRONGLY AGREE   AGREE   NEUTRAL   DISAGREE   STRONGLY DISAGREE

15) I feel I will be able to use what I learned through this process in other matters.

    STRONGLY AGREE   AGREE   NEUTRAL   DISAGREE   STRONGLY DISAGREE

Sometime it is erroneously assumed that lack of treatment fidelity on the consultee's part is due to a lack of skill; however, it is important to point out that low treatment integrity can be due to resistance or dissatisfaction with the consultation relationship. Thus, when faced with integrity issues it is important to take a measurement of the consultee's acceptability and reasons for resistance. Knoff (2013) points out that it is important to do a functional assessment of the consultee's resistance including determining if it is due to a lack of knowledge, lack of motivation, lack of acceptance of the consultation process, procedures, or approach, or lack of ability to generalize skills. Part of this functional assessment must be a social validity measure of the consultation process and the procedural recommendations.

ProtoFab Performance Improvement Project Continued

In addition to measuring the employees' on-time arrival at work and their cleanliness with respect to their work station and truck, social validity measures regarding the consultant were also assessed. The two owners and two upper-level managers (HR manager and ship manager), who had the most contact with the consultant, were asked to complete a social validity questionnaire and rate the consultant (1 = Very Little, 2, 3 = Some Extent, 4, 5 = Very Great Extent) on the following questions (Rodriguez, Sundberg, & Biagis, 2017):

- Looks at issues from a system's viewpoint with interrelated parts and how these interrelated parts influence one another.
- Perseveres and demonstrates rational judgement when confronted with adverse conditions.
- Maintains focus, quick to respond to questions with clear and concise answers based on data, provides leadership on process.
- Demonstrates confidence by leading in an assertive and innovative but respectful fashion, and a willingness to assume and defend a potentially unpopular and controversial position.
- Demonstrates strong personal ethics and values, evidenced by speaking candidly, following through on commitments, demonstrating respect for individuals and groups, and abiding by the spirt and intent of the organization's values and business ethics.
- Understands and discloses that she has knowledge and skill gaps and can learn from the experience and contributions of others, and is aware of and open about her own strengths and weaknesses and welcomes/solicits and uses feedback from others.
- Understands and considers the needs, issues, and motivation of others.
- Understands the optimal level of information needed to make things happen, constantly focused on the goal and proactively initiates pragmatic steps once information is available, in contrast to requiring extensive data or preparing elegant rather than practical solutions.

- Advocates her point of view and welcomes/solicits feedback, and is sincerely interested in others' opinions, sees merit in other's ideas and builds upon them.

In addition, three open ended questions were asked:

- What can I start doing to better support the organization's performance?
- What can I stop doing, that even though I may have good intentions, may not be in support of the organization's performance?
- What can I continue doing that adds value and is seen as a positive contribution to the organization, and to better support the organization's performance?
- Results are displayed in Figure 8.2 from the four who filled out the questionnaire. Some of the most interesting responses from the open-ended questions included: "Getting to know the frontline employees and having an understanding of what makes them tick would be helpful," "keep meetings simpler and shorter," "Keep holding everyone accountable," "I love that you are always positive… you never seem to get frustrated when we can't or don't want to follow" specific suggestions.

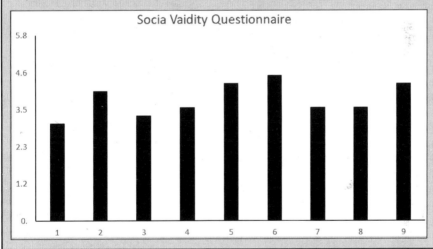

MEASURING AT THE CONSULTANT LEVEL

Just because the consultant is the one driving the boat *per se*, it does not mean that measurement at this level is not necessary. In fact, one could argue that if performance at that level is not effective, then the performance at the other two levels will fall apart. Treatment integrity of the consultation process has to do with whether consultation procedures were correctly used by the consultant. Although others have used a task-analysis of the consultation procedure to determine mastery of consultation skills during training (Kratochwioll, Elliot, & Busse, 1995); mastery during training should not be used as a measurement of a consultant's ability to consult. In fact, it can be argued that consultants need to continually engage in self-recording of consultation procedures and skills utilized during consultation as well as self-reflect on performance. The best way to achieve this requirement is to develop a task-analysis for each consultation session and for the consultant to self-record and self-graph adherence. Here is an example we developed for use during a consultation session during which the consultant is training the consultee on how to perform a specific procedure.

Assessing Consultation integrity – Training Session

Steps:	Completed	Not Completed	Comments
1) Address Consultee and check-in on what has happened since last visit			
2) Address consultee concerns			
3) Provide an overview of agenda			
4) Provide consultee opportunity to add to agenda			
5) Provide detailed instruction on procedure to be trained			
6) Check for understanding and questions			
7) Provide model of procedure to be trained			
8) Check for understanding and questions			
9) Set-up and conduct role-play			
10) Provide feedback on what consultee did correctly			
11) Provide feedback on incorrect performance and model correct performance			
12) Check for understanding and questions			
13) Repeat steps 9-12 until mastery			
14) Develop goals and objectives of how consultee will implement procedure			
15) Schedule next meeting			
16) End meeting and reinforce consultee's participation			
Total:			
Percentage (divide total by 16 X 100):			

When evaluating consultation, do not forget the importance of having done an assessment to determine to what degree you will need to interface with the medical profession. Ask yourself if the following have been completed:

- Evaluated client's medical history before considering interventions.
- Looked for behaviors and data patterns that may indicate medical origins of behavioral issues.
- If appropriate, use behavior strategies to teach and facilitate client's access to medical care.
- See the Appendix for a task analysis of the consultation process described in this book.

SUMMARY AND CONCLUSIONS

We recognize that as a consultant, you face many time pressures and are not always able to do a comprehensive evaluation. However, to demonstrate your effectiveness, you will want to use as many of the suggested applicable evaluation strategies as possible. The most important is to demonstrate change at the client level. Next is treatment fidelity and what is likely contributing to it, and finally, your own behavior and how you might improve upon it. Similar to developing objective measurement systems to capture client behavior, it will be important to develop and implement objective measurement systems at all levels of the consultation process: Client level, consultee level, and consultant level. This chapter provides some examples to incorporate into the consultation process, but the reader is encouraged to develop individual measurement systems based on the specifics of the consultation relationship. Remember—to be behavior analytic means to demonstrate behavior change, including in the consultation relationship.

ACTIVITIES

1. Describe how you are measuring the (a) client's, (b) consultee's, and (c) your behavior (the consultant's) to determine effectiveness.

Appendix

As with any task analysis, it is not meant to be used as in a rigid fashion. You often will need to add to and/or delete, modify, and rearrange steps depending on your situation. Also, you may find it helpful to elaborate on some of the major tasks we have listed here by breaking them down into smaller tasks. It is presented only as a rough guide, or checklist, to help you progress through the consultation process by checking off each task as you address it.

OVERVIEW OF CONSULTATION GOALS
(A CHECK-OFF LIST)

Phase 1: Develop A Collaborative Relationship

1. Begin to establish a professional working relationship and develop rapport. (Developing rapport and a professional relationship is an activity that permeates the entire consultation process.)
2. Conduct a multicultural assessment.
3. Identify behavior(s) of concern, operationalize and start an indirect A-B-C analysis on the client's targeted behavior as you are establishing a relationship.
4. Identify goal behavior(s) for client, operationalize and start A-B-C analysis from initial consultation session(s) with consultee. Cautionary note: Do not become the expert or the pair of hands.

5. Review client's complete medical history, listing of medications, any possible barriers to treatment (e.g., allergies, swallowing difficulties, other disabilities, etc.), and collaboratively determine if medical clearance might be necessary. If medical clearance or referrals are necessary, make at this time.
6. Arrange for observation of client's and consultee's behavior.
7. Identify sources of support for consultee's efforts.

Phase 2: Assess Current Situation[1]

1. Do, and/or supervise, a functional analysis of client's behavior (i.e., assess the maintaining contingencies supporting the behavior). If analysis indicates a possible medical basis for behavior, determine if a medical referral is appropriate.
2. Do a functional analysis of consultee's behavior (i.e., assess the maintaining contingencies supporting the behavior).
3. Consider doing a scatter plot.
4. Select observational and graphing methods and establish inter-observer reliability to help ensure observational accuracy for both the client's behavior and the consultee's behavior.
5. Measure (following adaptation and established reliability) and graph the target behavior (or supervise this activity) for your baseline measurement, again for both the client and consultee.
6. Identify barriers, if any, and implement sources of support for consultee's program implementation efforts.
7. While doing above observational assessments, continue to look for behaviors and data patterns that might indicate a medical basis for behavior issues, and determine if a medical referral is appropriate.

Phase 3: Discuss Possible Intervention

1. Discuss assessment results. Periodically review and discuss obtained results (data).
2. Discover what has been tried and if implemented appropriately[2].

---

[1] Additional assessments, such as a developmental assessment (e.g., Vineland) and/or a verbal assessment (e.g., *Early Echoic Skills Assessment, Verbal Behavior Milestones Assessment and Placement Program [VB-MAPP]*, or *Promoting the Emergence of Advanced Knowledge [PEAK]*) might also be used due to client needs and/or your organization's policy.

[2] For example, for reinforcement: Were high preference reinforcers selected? Were reinforcers applied frequently and immediately? Was the client given choices among high-preference reinforcers?

3. Jointly analyze possible contingencies (i.e., reinforcement or punishment) interfering with desired behavioral outcomes. Identify possible arbitrary reinforcers, including conducting a preference assessment.
4. Jointly develop intervention strategies for client and consultee that are contextually appropriate and evidence-based.
5. Consider planning an experimental design to evaluate treatment effectiveness.
6. Continue to identify and implement sources of support for consultee's efforts.

Phase 4: Implement the Intervention

1. Use behavioral skills training (BST) to assist consultee in learning how to accurately implement the intervention.
2. Consider implementing experimental design.
3. Jointly develop and apply strategies to facilitate program implementation fidelity, such as using a checklist.
4. Be present when intervention program is first implemented. Schedule fade out plan based upon accurate intervention implementation, effectiveness of intervention, and consultee's need for support.
5. Provide frequent feedback, reinforcing accurate program implementation.
6. Review and graph observational data on client's and consultee's behavior to monitor effects of intervention.
7. Continue to collect observational reliability periodically throughout intervention.
8. Program for generalization and maintenance.
9. Continue to identify and implement sources of support for consultee's efforts.

Phase 5: Monitor and Support Implementation Progress

1. Continue Steps 4 through 7 in Phase 4.
2. Involve others in reinforcing the implementation of the program by the consultee.
3. Assess treatment and consultation integrity.
4. Promote generalization of both the consultee's and client's target behaviors.

5. Continue to identify and implement sources of support for consultee's efforts.

Phase 6: Fix Anything that Has Gone Wrong

1. Use additional BST activities when treatment integrity needs improvement.
2. Correct for errors of omission or commission found in consultation assessment.
3. Assess for social validity and make any necessary changes.
4. Prompt others to reinforce consultee's program implementation as necessary.
5. Reassess for function(s) of behavior when necessary.
6. Continue to identify and implement sources of support for consultee's efforts.

Phase 7: Fade Out

1. Gradually phase out your support (prompts and reinforcers) for the program implementation as sources in the natural environment assume contingency control.
2. Assure generalization has occurred based on objective observation and data collection.
3. Continue collecting data to monitor both consultee and client behaviors and provide positive feedback as appropriate for maintenance and generalization.
4. For other behaviors needing to be addressed, operationalize them (problem behavior, if appropriate, and/or goal), then start at phase 2 and continue through phase 7.
5. Continue to identify and implement sources of support for consultee's efforts.

References

Albin, R. W., Lucyshyn, J. M., Horner, R. H., & Flannery, K. B. (1996). Contextual fit for behavioral support plans: A model for "goodness of fit." In L. K. Koegel, R. L. Koegel, & G. Dunlap (Eds), *Positive behavior support plans: Including people with difficult behavior in the community* (pp. 81–98). Baltimore: Brookes.

Allen, K. D., & Wallace, D. P. (2013). Effectiveness of using noncontingent escape for general behavior management in a pediatric dental clinic. *Journal of Applied Behavior Analysis, 46*(4): 723–737.

Alvero, A. M., Bucklin, B. R., & Austin, J. (2001). An objective review of the effectiveness and essential characteristics of performance feedback in organizational settings (1985–1998). *Journal of Organizational Behavior Management, 21*(1), 3–29.

Arco, L. (1997). Improving program outcome with process-based performance feedback. *Journal of Organizational Behavior Management, 17*(1), 37–64. Retrieved from http://mimas.calstatela.edu/login?url=https://search.proquest.com/docview/199260675?accountid=10352

Bacon, D. L., Fulton, J. J., & Malott, R. W. (1982). Improving staff performance through the use of task checklists. *Journal of Organizational Behavior Management, 4*(1), 17–25.

Barbetta, P. M., Heron, T. E., & Heward, W. L. (1993). Effects on active student response during error correction on the acquisition, maintenance, and developmental disabilities. *Journal of Applied Behavior Analysis, 26,* 111–119. doi: 10.1901/jaba.1993.26=11

Barton, E. J., & Bevirt, J. (1981). Generalization of sharing across groups: Assessment of group composition with preschool children. *Behavior Modification, 5,* 503–522.

Beaulieu, L., Hanley, G. P., & Roberson, A. A. (2013). Effects of peer mediation on preschoolers' compliance and compliance precursors. *Journal of Applied Behavior Analysis, 46,* 555–567 doi: 10.1002/jaba.66

Behavior Analysis Certification Board. (2017). BACB Professional and Ethical Compliance Code for Behavior Analysts. Retrieved from https://www.bacb.com/ethics/ethics-code/

Berger, S. M., & Ludwig, T. D. (2007). Reducing warehouse employee errors using voice-assisted technology that provided immediate feedback. *Journal of Organizational Behavior Management, 27*(1), 1–31.

REFERENCES

Binder, C. (1994). Measurably superior instructional methods: Do we need sales and marketing? In R. Gardner, III., D. M. Sainato, J. O. Cooper, T. E. Heron, W. L. Heward, J. Eshleman, & T. A. Grossi (Eds). *Behavior analysis in education: Focus on measurably superior instruction* (pp. 21–31.

Boyce, T. E., & Geller, E. S. (2001). Applied behavior analysis and occupational safety: The challenge of response maintenance. *Journal of Organizational Behavior Management, 21,* 31–60.

Braukmann, C. J., Maloney, D. M., Fixsen, D. L., Phillips, E. L., & Wolf, M. M. (1974). An analysis of a selection interview training package for predelinquents at achievement place. *Criminal Justice and Behavior, 1,* 30–42.

Brodhead, M. T. (2019). Culture always matters: Some thoughts on Rosenberg and Schwartz. *Behavior Analysis in Practice, 12,* 826–830.

Brunsting, N. C., Sreckovic, M. A., & Lane, K. L. (2014). Special education teacher burnout: A synthesis of research from 1979 to 2013. *Education and Treatment of Children, 37,* 681–712.

Buehler, R. E., Patterson, G. R., & Furness, J. M. (1966). The reinforcement of behavior in institutional settings. *Behavior Research and Therapy, 4,* 157–167.

Burg, M. M., Reid, D. H., & Lattimore, J. (1979). Use of a self-recording and supervision program to change institutional staff behavior. *Journal of Applied Behavior Analysis, 12,* 363–375.

Caldarella, P., Larsen, R. A. A., Williams, L., Wills, H. P., & Wehby, J. H. (2019). Teacher praise-to-reprimand ratios: Behavioral response of students at risk for EBD compared with typically developing peers. *Education and Treatment of Children, 42,* 447–468.

California Department of Health Care Services, 2013L Authorization for Release of Patient Information, California Department of Health Care Services. Retrieved from: https://www.dhcs.ca.gov/formsandpubs/forms/Forms/Mental_Health/DHCS_1811.pdf

Cancio, E. J., Albrecht, S. F., & Johns, B. H. (2013). Defining administrative support and its relationship to the attrition of teachers of students with emotional and behavioral disorders. *Education and Treatment of Children, 36,* 71–94.

Cannella-Malone, H., Sigafoos, J., O'Reilly, M., De la Cruz, B., Edrisinha, C., & Lancioni, G. (2006). Comparing Video Prompting to Video Modeling for Teaching Daily Living Skills to Six Adults with Developmental Disabilities. *Education and Training in Developmental Disabilities, 41*(4), 344–356

Carr, E. G., (1996). The transfiguration of behavior analysis: Strategies for survival. *Journal of Behavioral Education, 6,* 263–270.

Carroll, R. A., Kodak, T., & Fisher, W. W. (2013). An evaluation of programmed treatment-integrity errors during discrete trial instruction. *Journal of Applied Behavior Analysis, 46,* 379–394.

Carroll, R. A., Owsiany, J., & Cheatham, J. M. (2018). Using an abbreviated assessment to identify effective error-correction procedures for individual learners during discrete-trial instruction. *Journal of Applied Behavior Analysis, 51,* 482–501. https://doe.org/10.1002/jaba.460

Chez, M. (2008). *Autism and its medical management.* London & Philadelphia: Jesica Kingsley Publishers.

Clement, P. W. (1972, Oct.) Parents, peers, and child patients make the best therapists. Paper presented at the 4th Annual Southern California Conference on Behavior Modification, Los Angeles.

Codding, R. S., Feinberg, A. B., Dunn, E. K., & Pace, G. M. (2005). Effects of immediate performance feedback on implementation of behavior support plans. *Journal of Applied Behavior Analysis, 38,* 205–219.

Codding, R. S., Livanis, A., Pace, G. M., & Vaca, L. (2008). Using performance feedback to improve treatment integrity of classwide behavior plans: An investigation of observer reactivity. *Journal of Applied Behavior Analysis, 41,* 417–422.

Coles, E., & Blunden, R. (1981). Maintaining new procedures using feedback to staff, a hierarchical reporting system, and a multidisciplinary management group. *Journal of Organizational Behavior Management, 3,* 19–33.

Cook, C. R., Grady, E. A., Long, A. C., Renshaw, R., Codding, R. S., Fiat, A., & Larson, M. (2016). Evaluating the impact of increasing general education teachers ratio of positive-to-negative interactions on students' classroom behavior. *Journal of Positive Behavior Interventions, 18,* 1–11. doi: 10: 1177/1098300716679137

Cook, C. R., Mayer, G. R., Browning-Wright, D., Kraemer, B., Wallace, M., Dart, E., & Collins, T. (2010). Exploring the link between evidence-based behavior intervention plans and student outcomes: An initial effectiveness study. *The Journal of Special Education, 41* (Published online before print, May, 2010. http://sed.sagepub.com/content/early/2010)

Copeland, L. E., & Buch, G. (2019). Addressing Medical Issues in Behavior Analytic Treatment. *Behavior Analysis in Practice.* Feb, 2019. DOI: 10.1007/s40617-019-00342–9

Cormier, W. H., & Cormier, L. S. (1979). *Interviewing strategies for helpers: A guide to assessment, treatment, and evaluation.* Monterey, CA: Brooks/Cole Publishing Co.

Corrigan, P. W., William, O. B., McCracken, S. G., Kommana, S., Edwards, M., & Brunner, J. (1998). Staff attitudes that impede the implementation of behavioral treatment programs. *Behavior Modification, 22,* 548–562.

Cossairt, A., Hall, R. V., & Hopkins, B. L. (1973). The effects of experimenter's instructions, feedback, and praise on teacher praise and student attending behavior. *Journal of Applied Behavior Analysis, 6,* 89–100.

Craft, M. A., Alber, S. R., & Heward, W. L. (1998). Teaching elementary students with developmental disabilities to recruit teacher attention in a general education classroom: Effects on teacher praise and academic productivity. *Journal of Applied Behavior Analysis, 31,* 399–415.

Critchfield, T. S. (2017). Visuwords®: a handy online tool for estimating what non experts may think when hearing behavior analysis jargon. *Behavior Analysis in Practice, 10,* 318–322.

Critchfield, T. S., Doepke, K. J., Epting, L. K., Becirevic, A., Reed, D. D., Fienup, D. M., Kremsreiter, J. L., & Scott, C. L. (2017). Normative emotional responses to behavior analysis jargon or how not to use words to win friends and influence people. *Behavior Analysis in Practice, 10,* 97–106.

Crone, D. A., Hawken, L. S., & Bergstrom, M. K. (2007). A demonstration of training, implementing and using functional assessment in 10 elementary and middle school settings. *Journal of Positive Behavior Intervention, 9,* 15–29.

D'Andrea, M., & Daniels, J. (2001). RESPECTFUL counseling: An integrative model for counselors. In D. Pope-Davis & H. Coleman (Eds.), *The interface of class, culture, and gender in counseling* (pp. 417–466). Thousand Oaks, CA: Sage.

Deleon, I. G., Hagopian, L. P., Rodruguez-Catter, V., Bowman, L. G., Long, E. S., & Boelter, E. W. (2008). Increasing wearing prescription glasses in individuals with mental retardation. *Journal of Applied Behavior Analysis.* 41(1): 137–142

Dengerink, K. (2013, Mater's project at San Diego State Univ.) Parent training: The effects of in-home coaching following workshops in Huaycan, Peru.

Dennison, A., Laund, E. M., Brodhead, M. T., Jejia, L., Armenta, A., & Leal, J. (2019). Delivering home-supported applied behavior analysis therapies to culturally and linguistically diverse families. *Behavior Analysis in Practice, 12,* 887–898.

DeRicco, D. A., & Niemann, J. E. (1980). In vivo effects of peer modeling on drinking rate. *Journal of Applied Behavior Analysis, 13,* 149–152.

DiGennaro, F. D., Martens, B. K., & Kleinmann, A. E. (2007). A comparison of performance feedback procedures on teachers' treatment implementation integrity and students' inappropriate behavior in special education classrooms. *Journal of Applied Behavior Analysis, 40,* 447–461.

DiGennaro-Reed, F. D., Codding, R., Catania, C. N., & Maguire, H. (2010). Effects of video modeling on treatment integrity of behavioral interventions. *Journal of Applied Behavior Analysis, 43(2),* 291–295.

DiGennaro-Reed, F. D., Reed, D. D., Baez, C. N., & Maguire, H. (2011). A parametric analysis of errors of commission during discrete-trial training. *Journal of Applied Behavior Analysis, 44(3),* 611–615.

Dustin, R. (1974). Training for institutional change. *The Personnel and Guidance Journal, 52,* 422–427.

Farber, H. & Mayer, G. R. (1972). Behavior consultation in a barrio high school. *The Personnel and Guidance Journal, 51,* 273–279.

Fong, E. H., Catagnus, R., Brodhead, M., Quigley, S., & Field, S. (2016). Developing the cultural awareness skills of behavior analysts. *Behavior Analysis in Practice, 9,* 84–94.

Freshman, B. (2016). Cultural competency: Best intentions are not good enough. *Diversity and Equality in Health Care, 13,* 240–244.

Frying, M. J., Wallace, M. D., & Yassine, J. N. (2012). Impact of treatment integrity on intervention effectiveness. *Journal of Applied Behavior Analysis, 45,* 449–453. doi: 10.1901/jaba.2012.45-449.

Gallessich, J. (1973). Organizational factors influencing consultation in schools. *Journal of School Psychology, 11,* 57–65.

Gersten, R., Keating, T., Yovanoff, P., & Harniss, M. K. (2001). Working in special education: Factors that enhance special educators' intent to stay. *Exceptional Children, 67,* 549–567.

Gillat, A., & Sulzer-Azaroff, B. (1994). Promoting principals managerial involvement in institutional improvement. *Journal of Applied Behavior Analysis, 27,* 115–129.

Goings, K., Carr, L., Maguire, H., Harper, J. M., & Luiselli, J. K. (2019). Improving classroom appearance and organization through supervisory performance improvement intervention. *Behavior Analysis in Practice, 12,* 430–434.

Graubard, P. S., Rosenberg, H., & Miller, M. B. (1971). Student applications of behavior modification to teachers and environments or ecological approaches to social deviancy. In E. A. Ramp & B. L. Hopkins (Eds.). *A new direction for education: Behavior Analysis, 1971.* (pp. 80–101). Lawrence, Kansas: University of Kansas.

Heinicke, M. R., & Carr, J. E. (2014). Applied Behavior Analysis in acquired brain injury rehabilitation. A meta-analysis of single-case design intervention research. *Behavioral Interventions.* 29, 77–105.

Holden, B., & Sulzer-Azaroff, B. (1972). Schedules of follow-up and their effect upon the maintenance of a prescriptive teaching program. In Semb, G., Green, I. R., Hawkins, R. P., Michael, J., Phillips, E. L., Sherman, J. A., Sloane, H., & Thomas, D. R. (Eds.) *Behavior analysis and education.* Kansas: University of Kansas.

Horner, R. H. (1994). Functional assessment: Contributions and future directions. *Journal of Applied Behavior Analysis, 27,* 401–404.

Hunt, S., & Sulzer-Azaroff, B. (1974). *Motivating parent participation in home training sessions with pre-trainable retardants.* Paper presented at the American Psychological Association, New Orleans, Louisiana.

Ivey, A. E., Ivey, M. B., Zalaquett, C. P. (2018). *Intentional interviewing and counseling: facilitating client development in a multicultural society*. Boston, MA: Cengage Learning.

Iwata, B. A., Zarcone, J. R., Vollmer, T. R., & Smith, R. G. (1994). Assessment and treatment of self-injurious behavior. In E. Schopler & G.B. Mesibov (Eds). Behavioral Issues in Autism (pp.129–157). NY: Plenum Press.

John, S., & Brown, R. (1969). Producing behavior change in parents of disturbed children. *Journal of Child Psychology and Psychiatry, 10,* 107–121.

Johnson, C. A., & Katz, R. C. (1973). Using parents as change agents for their children: A review. *The Journal of Child Psychology and Psychiatry, 14,* 181–200. https: //doe.org/10.1111/j.1469–7610.1973.tb01186.x

Kaiser, L., Rosenfield, S., & Gravois, T. (2009). Teachers' perception of satisfaction, skill development, and skill application after instructional consultation services. *Journal of Learning Disabilities, 42,* 444–57.

Knoff, H. M. (2013). Changing resistant consultees: Functional assessment leading to strategic intervention. *Journal of Educational and Psychological Consultation, 23,* 307–317.

Kodak, T., Campbell, V., Bergmann, S., LeBlanc, B., Kurtz-Nelson, E., Cariveau, T., Haq, S., Semantik, P., & Mahon, J. (2016). Examination of efficacious, efficient, and socially valid error-correction procedures to teach sight words and prepositions to children with autism spectrum disorder. *Journal of Applied Behavior Analysis, 49,* 532–547. doi: 10.1002/jaba.310

Koffler, T, Ushakov K., & Avraham K. (2015). Genetics of Hearing Loss-Syndromic. *Otolaryngologic Clinics, 48*(6): 1041–1061.

Kopelman, R. E., & Schneller, G. O. (1981). A mixed-consequence system for reducing overtime and unscheduled absences. *Journal of Organizational Behavior Management, 3*(1), 17–28. https://doi-org.mimas.calstatela.edu/10.1300/J075v03n01_02

Kratochwill, T. R., Elliott, S. N., & Busse, R. T. (1995). Behavior consultation: A five-year evaluation of consultant and client outcomes. *School Psychology Quarterly, 10*(2), 87–117. https://doi-org.mimas.calstatela.edu/10.1037/h0088299

Krumboltz, J. D., & Krumboltz, H. G. (1972). *Changing children's behavior.* Englewood Cliffs, NJ: Prentice-Hall.

Krumboltz, J. D., & Thoresen, C. E. (1964). The effects of behavioral counseling in groups and individual settings on information seeking behavior. *Journal of Counseling Psychology, 11,* 324–333.

Lane, J., Lee, H., Smith, L., et al. (2011). Clinical severity and quality of life in children and adolescents with Rett syndrome. *Neurology,* 77, 1812–1818.

LeBlanc, L.A., Heinicke, M. R., & Baker, J. C. (2012). Expanding the Consumer Base for Behavior Analytic Services: Meeting the Needs of Consumers in the 21st Century. *Behavior Analysis in Practice, 5,* 4–14.

Leland, W., & Stockwell, A. (2019). A self-assesment tool for cultivating affirming practices with transgender and gender-nonconforming (TGNC) clients, supervisees, students and colleagues. *Behavior Analysis in Practice, 12,* 816–825.

Lisabethe, L. D, Brown, D. L., Hughes, R., et al. (2009). Acute Stroke Symptoms: Comparing Women and Men. *Stroke*; 40:2031–2036

Loeber, R. (1971). Engineering the behavioral engineer. *Journal of Applied Behavior Analysis, 4,* 321–326.

MacDonald, W. S., Gallimore, R., & MacDonald, G. (1970). Contingency counseling by school personnel: An economical model of intervention. *Journal of Applied Behavior Analysis, 3,* 175–182.

Mangiapanello, K. A., & Hemmes, N. S. (2015). An analysis of feedback from a behavior analytic perspective. *Behavior Analyst, 38,* 51–75. DOI: 10.1007/s40614-014-0026-x

Martin, J. A. (1974, August). *Children's task preferences: Effects of reinforcement and punishment.* Paper presented at the meeting of the American Psychological Association, New Orleans.

Mayer, G. R. (1972). Behavioral consulting: Using behavior modification procedures in the consulting relationship. *Elementary School Guidance and Counseling, 7,* 114–119.

Mayer, G. R. (2000). *Classroom Management: A California resource guide.* Los Angeles County Office of Education Safe Schools. Downey, CA.

Mayer, G. R. (2020). *The positive classroom: Improving student learning and behavior.* Cornwall-on-Hudson, NY: Sloan Publishing.

Mayer, G. R., Butterworth, T., Komoto, T., & Benoit, R. (1983). The influence of the school principal on the consultant's effectiveness. *Elementary School Guidance & Counseling, 17,* 274–279.

Mayer, G. R., Butterworth, T., Nafpaktitis, M., & Sulzer-Azaroff, B. (1983). Preventing school vandalism and improving discipline: A three-year study. *Journal of Applied Behavior Analysis, 16,* 355–369.

Mayer, G. R., & McGookin, R. B. (1977). *Behavioral consulting.* Los Angeles, CA.: Office of the Los Angeles County Superintendent of Schools.

Mayer, G. R., Mitchell, L., Clementi, T., Clement-Robertson, E., Myatt, R., & Bullara, D. T. (1993). A dropout prevention program for at-risk high school students: Emphasizing consulting to promote positive classroom climates. *Education and Treatment of Children, 16,* 135–146.

Mayer, G. R., Sulzer-Azaroff, B., & Wallace, M. (2019). *Behavior analysis for lasting change, 4th Ed.* Cornwall-on-Hudson, NY: Sloan Publishing.

Mazaleski, J. L., Iwata, B. A., Vollmer, T. R., Zarcone, J. R., & Smith, R. G. (1993). Analysis of the reinforcement and extinction components in DRO contingencies with self-injury. *Journal of Applied Behavior Analysis, 26,* 143–156.

McComas, J. J., Wacker, D. P., & Cooper, L. J. (1998). Increasing compliance with medical procedures: application of the high-probability request procedure to a toddler. *Journal of Applied Behavior Analysis,* 31(2). 287–290.

McGhan, A. C., & Lerman, D. C. (2013). An assessment of error-correction procedures for learners with autism. *Journal of Applied Behavior Analysis, 46,* 626–639. DOI: 10.1002/jaba.65

McIntosh, K., Predy, L. K., Upreti, G., Hume, A. E., Turri, M. G., & Mathews, S. (2014). Perceptions of contextual features related to implementation and sustainability of school-wide positive behavior support. *Journal of Positive Behavior Interventions, 16,* 31–43.

Minor, L., DuBard, M., & Luiselli, J. K. (2014). Improving intervention integrity of direct service practitioners through performance feedback and problem solving consultation. *Behavioral Interventions, 29,* 145–156. doi: 10.1002/bin.1382

Montegar, C. A., Reid, D. H., Madsen, C. H., & Ewell, M. D. (1977). Increasing institutional staff to resident interactions through inservice training and supervisor approval. *Behavior Therapy, 8,* 533–540.

Mortenson, B. P., & Witt, J. C. (1998). The use of weekly performance feedback to increase teacher implementation of a prereferral academic intervention. *School Psychology Review, 27,* 613–627.

Mouzakitis, A., Codding, R. S., & Tryon, G. (2015). The effects of self-monitoring and performance feedback on the treatment integrity of behavior intervention plan implementation and generalization. *Journal of Positive Behavior Interventions, 17,* 223–234. DOI: 10.1177/1098300715573629 jpbi.sagepub.com

Mozingo, D. B., Smith, T., Riodan, M. R., Reiss, M. L., & Bailey, J. S. (2006). Enhancing frequency recording by developmental disabilities treatment staff. *Journal of Applied Behavior Analysis, 39,* 253–256.

Muller, M. M., Piazza, C. C., Moore, J. W., Kelley, M. E., Bethke, S. A., Pruett, A. E., et al. (2003). Training parents to implement pediatric feeding protocols. *Journal of Applied Behavior Analysis, 36,* 545–562.

Newhouse-Oisten M., Peck K., Conway A., Frieder J. (2017). Ethical Considerations for Interdisciplinary Collaboration with Prescribing Professionals. *Behav Anal Pract.* 10(2): 145–153

Noell, G. H., Gresham, F. M., & Gansle, K. A. (2002). Does treatment integrity matter? A preliminary investigation of instructional implementation and mathematics performance. *Journal of Behavioral Education, 11,* 51–61.

Noell, G., Witt, J., LaFleur, L., Mortenson, B., Ranier, D., & LeVelle, J. (2000). Increasing Intervention implementation in general education following consultation: A comparison of two follow-up strategies. *Journal of Applied Behavior Analysis, 33*(3), 271–284.

O'Reilly, M. (1997). Functional Analysis of episodic self-injury correlated with recurrent otitis media. *Journal of Applied Behavior Analysis, 30,* 165–167.

Patterson, G. R., Littman, R. A., & Bricker, W. (1967). Assertive behavior in children: A step toward a theory of aggression. *Monographs for Society of Research in Child Development, 32,* 1–38.

Pelios, L., Morren, J., Tesch, D., & Axelrod, S. (1999). The impact of functional analysis methodology on treatment choice for self-injurious and aggressive behavior. *Journal of Applied Behavior Analysis, 32,* 185–195.

Petscher, E. S., & Bailey, J. S. (2006). Effect of training, prompting, and self-monitoring on staff behavior in a classroom for students with disabilities. *Journal of Applied Behavior Analysis, 39,* 215–226.

Phaneuf, L. J., & McIntyre, L. L. (2007). Effects of individualized video feedback combined with group parent training on inappropriate maternal behavior. *Journal of Applied Behavior Analysis, 40,* 737–741.

Piazza, C. C. (2008). Feeding disorders and behavior: What have we learned? *Developmental Disabilities Research Reviews, 14*(2), 174–181.

Poche, C., Brouwer, R., & Swearingen, M. (1981). Teaching self-protection to young children. *Journal of Applied Behavior Analysis, 14,* 169–176.

Porter, E. H. (1950). *An introduction to therapeutic counseling.* Boston: Houghton Mifflin Co

Rasmussen, E. B., & Newland. M. C. (2008). Asymmetry of reinforcement and punishment in human choice. *Journal of the Experimental Analysis of behavior, 89,* 157–167.

Richling S. M., Rapp J. T., Carroll R. A., et al. (2011). Using noncontingent reinforcement to increase compliance with wearing prescription prostheses. *Journal of Applied Behavior Analysis, 44*(2): 375–379.

Ringer, V. M. J. (1973). The use of a "token helper" in the management of classroom behavior problems and in teacher training. *Journal of Applied Behavior Analysis, 6,* 671–677.

Robinson, N., & St. Peter, C. C. (2019). Accumulated reinforcers increase academic responding and suppress problem behave for students with Attention-Deficit Hyperactivity Disorder. *Journal of Applied Behavior Analysis, 52,* 1076–1088. doi:10.1002/jaba.570.

Rodriguez, M., Sundberg, D., & Biagis. (2017). *OBM applied! A practical guide to implementing organizational behavior management (Vol.4).* Melbourne, FL: ABA Technologies, Inc.

Rosenfield, S. (1991). The relationship variable in behavioral consultation. *Journal of Behavioral Consulting, 1,* 329–336.

Sanetti, L. M. H., & Kratochwill, T. R. (2007). Treatment integrity in behavioral consultation: Measurement, promotion, and outcomes. *International Journal of Behavioral Consultation and Therapy*, 4, *95–144.*

Schein, E. (1999). *Process consultation revisited: Building the helping relationship.* Reading, MA: Addison-Wesley.

Seeman, H. (1994). *Preventing classroom discipline problems: A guide for educators (2nd. Ed.).* Lancaster, PA: Technomic Publishing Co.

Sheridan, S. M., Witte, A. L., Holmes, S. R., Coutts, M. J., Dent, A. L., Kunz, G. M., & Wu, C. (2017). A randomized trial examining the effects of Conjoint Behavioral Consultation in rural schools: Student outcomes and the mediating role of the teacher-parent relationship. *Journal of School Psychology*, *61*, 33–53.

Sherman, T. M., & Cormier, W. H. (1974). An investigation of the influence of student behavior on teacher behavior. *Journal of Applied Behavior Analysis, 7,* 11–21.

Skinner, B. F. (1981). Selection by consequences. *Science*, *213*, 501–504.

St. Peter Pipkin, C., Vollmer, T. R., & Sloman, K. N. (2010). Effects of treatment integrity failures during differential reinforcement of alternative behavior: A translational model. *Journal of Applied Behavior Analysis*, *43(1)*, 47–70.

Sugai, G., & Horner, R. H. (1999). Discipline and behavioral support: Preferred processes and practices. *Effective School Practices, 17*(4), 10–22.

Sweigart, C. A., Landrum, T. J., & Pennington, R. C. (2015). The effects of real-time visual performance feedback on teacher feedback: A preliminary investigation. *Education and Treatment of Children, 38,* 429–450.

Taber, T. A., Lambright, N., & Luiselli, J. K. (2017). Video modeling training effects on types of attention delivered by educational care-providers. *Behavior Analysis in Practice, 10,* 189–194.

Taylor, D. V., Rush, D., Hetrick, W. P., & Sandman, C. A. (1993). Self-injurious behavior within the menstrual cycle of women with mental retardation. *American Journal on Mental Retardation*, 24: 331–344.

Taylor, W. F., & Hoedt, K. C. (1974). Classroom-related behavior problems: Counsel parents, teachers, or children?

Whitaker, S. D. (2000). Mentoring beginning special education teachers and the relationship to attrition. *Exceptional Children, 66,* 546–566.

Williams, W. L. (2000). Behavioral consultation. In J. Austin & J. E. Carr (Eds.), *Handbook of applied behavior analysis* (pp. 375–397). Reno, NV: Context Press.

Wright, P. I. (2019). Cultural humility in th practice of applied behavior analysis. *Behavior Analysis in Practice, 12,* 805–809.

Worsdell, A. S., Iwata, B. A., Hanley, G. P., Thompson, R. H., & Kahng, S. W. (2000). Effects of continuous and intermittent reinforcement for problem behavior during functional communication training. *Journal of Applied Behavior Analysis, 33,* 167–179.

Zarcone, J., Brodhead, M., & Tarbox, J. (2019). Beyond a call to action: An introduction to the special issue on diversity and equity in the practice of behavior analysis. *Behavior Analysis in Practice*, 12, 741–742.

Zimmerman, B. J., & Rosenthal, T. L. (1974). Observational learning of rule-governed behavior by children. *Psychological Bulletin, 81,* 29–42.

Zuckerman, K. E., Lindly, O. J., Reyes, N. M., Chavez, A. E., Macias, K., Smith, K. N., & Reynolds, A. (2017). Disparities in diagnosis and treatment of autism in Latino and non-Latino White families. *Pediatrics, 139,* 1–10.